DATE DUE

English for a Successful Life in the USA

English for a Successful Life in the USA

A workbook of advice for ESL students

By the ESL students of TALK International and the Nova English Program in Florida

Writers Club Press

San Jose New York Lincoln Shanghai

English for a Successful Life in the USA
A workbook of advice for ESL students

Writers Club Press
an imprint of iUniverse.com, Inc.

For information address:
iUniverse.com, Inc.
5220 S 16th, Ste. 200
Lincoln, NE 68512
www.iuniverse.com

ISBN: 0-595-18601-7

Printed in the United States of America

For everyone who wants to live in the USA.

Contents

A list of internet pages that are used in this workbook
www.geocities.com/talkinternational/conversation.html (Here are some hints for making conversations easy and fun)

www.geocities.com/novanewspaper/page1.html
(The newspaper that the students at Nova English School started in November 2000)

www.geocities.com/countries2001/instruction.html (a how-to sheet for using geocities.com, a web-based program for making web pages)

www.teacherstoteachers.com (This page has links to the activities of several teachers who want you to enjoy learning English. Show these pages to your teacher and help them make English classes more fun!)

www.talkinusa.com (This web page has a link to a monthly practice page)

www.angelfire.com/fl4/goodidea/ (This is a website that collects suggestions and advice)

www.geocities.com/countries2001/index.html (This page is a starting point for learning about other cultures. There is also a link to a list of grammar practice pages)

The easiest way to navigate to these sites is to do the following: (1) go to *www.teacherstoteachers.com*. (2) click on ESL BOOK. (3) look for "LINKS" on the ESL Book's Table of Contents. (4) the links will be listed to all of the web pages mentioned in this book.

Foreword

ESL means English for a Successful Life in the USA

This book is for all students of English as a Second Language (ESL). It is a collection of suggestions and stories about the experiences of students who came to the USA before you. We want you to learn English for a Successful Life in the USA.

The exercises and most of the readings were written for intermediate and advanced students of English. There are special additional exercises that will be very challenging for advanced students. These are usually indicated with the words "More Exercises."

If you are an advanced student and you want more work related to this book, go to www.geocities.com/talkinternational/contents.html and you will find a lot of additional exercises. You can reach this site by going to www.teacherstoteachers.com and then click on "ESL BOOK" (or go to *www.whatdoyaknow.com*). If you are a beginner, there is space on each page for your teacher to explain difficult words and help you understand.

Please read the first ten pages today. You can read any part of this book in any order (after the ten pages). We hope you will also look at Chapter 13: Stress.

Teachers to Teachers Books
www.teacherstoteachers.com

2455 East Sunrise Blvd., Suite 200, Fort Lauderdale, FL 33304
Send comments about this book to englishlesson@mail.com
954.565.8505
Fax 954.565.8718
www.talkinusa.com

This book will never go out of date. We will put updates to this book on our website. You can visit the website in two ways. If you like to type a lot, you can go directly to the website at: www.geocities.com/talkinternational/contents.html

If you want to click, go to *www.teacherstoteachers.com* and CLICK on "English for Successful Living"

Teachers to Teachers is a supporter of the "Every Country Tour" by Gustavo Woltmann. You can see more by clicking on "140 Countries" on the website. You can also practice English by writing to alohatraveler@hotmail.com.

This book is available from major book vendors (it was published by iUniverse.com). Each chapter is supplemented with photos on web sites. You are buying more than a book. You have in your hands a complete system for practicing and improving your English.
a) You can write to the authors of this book and learn more.
b) You can look up photos at www.teachrestoteachers.com and then click on ESL BOOK.
c) You can send your compositions to the webmaster and you composition will be corrected and posted on the web site.
d) You can find useful advice to help you with your new life in the USA

NOTE: The focus of this book is on Florida. This book's suggestions are also helpful in other parts of the USA. Students who want more information about useful information in other parts of the USA can write to us and we'll post more information on the web site.

Acknowledgements

Many thanks to my colleagues at TALK International School of Languages and Nova Southeastern University's English Language Program. Our interaction helped to shape this book. Specific thanks to Barbara, Dean, Rebecca, George, Carrie, Maja, Martha, Leslie, Vivian, Cary, Des, Marta, Marlen, Elizabeth, Ale, Krista, Tony, John, Paul, Catherine, Sidnoise, Gary, Cheryl, and other teachers I've worked with.

List of Contributors

(They encourage you to write to them with your comments and questions)

The students of the ESL program at Nova

Sandra Avila, Alejandro (the architect) *ahiquera56@hotmail.com*, Alejandro (the graphic artist) *alejandrofilippi@aol.com*, Dr. Daniela, *danibabe81@hotmail.com*, Coco Daniela, Roxana, Maria Cecilia, Maria Carolina, Elsy, elsycampos@yahoo.com, Lina, Woo Young Kwon, Sandra, Francisco Mella, Beatriz.

There are more e-mail addresses at the ESL BOOK website.

The students at the EFL program at TALK International in Fort Lauderdale

Benjamin (the floorball expert), Pi-Ying piying1004@hotmail.com, Alex, alexis_salfatte@hotmail.com (call him to practice your telephone English. He also hosts a Wednesday evening with "popcorn and a movie" to discuss US culture with a teacher. Please come around 7 p.m. Call 954.646.8246 to see if the meeting has been moved or changed. Visit www.teacherstoteachers.com and click on "Culture Night at Alex's House")

The photos of the contributors appear in the ESL Book web site, which you can visit by going to *www.teacherstoteachers.com*, then you click on "ESL BOOK" and then click on "Contributors."

Special thanks to the people who sent their contributions to this book by e-mail. You saved my fingers with your keystrokes.

Two trees were planted in a tropical country when you purchased this book. The tree-planting program is Trees for the Future www.treesftf.org and the tree that was planted will absorb more than one ton of carbon dioxide over the next 40 years. That's enough to off-set the carbon dioxide that was emitted to produce and distribute this book.

Introduction

Welcome! We want to welcome you to the USA. (If you are reading this in another country, we hope you will visit the USA soon!)

We want you to be safe and to have a good life in the USA, so we have created a list of important things to remember…

READ THIS PAGE FIRST

The Ten Most Important Things
What should a new student bring to the USA?
1. Postcards, posters and brochures from your country.
2. Recipes for special and typical meals from your country.
3. Photos of your family (in class, you will talk about your brothers and sisters).
4. Maps of your city.
5. A picture book or photo tour book of your city.
6. Photos of your dog or cat.
7. Interesting videos about your country (Carnival if you are from Brazil, Oktoberfest if you are from Germany, etc.).
8. Music (on CD or cassette) that is typical of your country (we play music to signal the end of the class).
9. News from your country (newspapers, magazines, recordings from the radio and videos of TV news) so that you can translate current events to your classmates.
10. Some jokes.

What should new students know when they arrive in the USA?

SPECIAL INFORMATION FOR South Florida

1. Sharks swim near the coast at night. NEVER swim in the ocean at night!

2. Florida is the lightning capital of the world. Lightning can strike at an angle. The sky does not need to be dark above you.

3. Some parts of South Florida are dangerous-do not stay for a long time near most parts of I-95.

4. Be careful if you buy electronic products (especially in Downtown Miami). The prices are often low because the equipment is out of date or not equipped with all of the correct software. Something is usually missing or different in some of the stores in Miami. You need to ask, "Where is the warranty card?" Some of the boxes have been opened, something has been changed, and then the box has been resealed.

5. POLICE: If a police officer stops your car, please keep your hands (BOTH hands) on the steering wheel. If your windows have dark tinting, roll down the window and put both hands back on the wheel. If you think the officer is not a real officer, shout to him that you are moving slowly to a public place. Then move slowly with your lights blinking to show that you are not running away. (If you have questions about this, please talk with your teacher or write to a student. It's important that the police officer knows that you are not running away, so write this note: "I want to move to a public place." If he doesn't agree, perhaps he is not a police officer.)

6. Talk to strangers (they are a good source of new words). Unfortunately, you need to look out when you are bicycling. Some robbers push a bicycle rider on the ground and then take the bicycle. Be careful about which strangers you talk to. In general, if you smile at a stranger, the person will be surprised (since many U.S. people who live in cities don't smile at strangers).

7. Attention! There are many pickpockets, especially at Sawgrass Mills Mall.

8. It is important to carry a cell phone number. Call 954-565-8505 (the phone number of TALK School) and ask politely, "I am a student of English. I need some advice or suggestions about the best cell phone service." If you are polite and patient, then usually someone in the USA will help you!

9. Always speak slowly and clearly. Carry paper so you can write your question on paper (perhaps the US speaker does not understand your accent). The paper will also be useful for other people to use to give you information.

Other Interesting Information
PRACTICE TALKING AT A FREE EVENING CLASS
TALK International School has a weekly dinner at a student's house. In 2001, the host student is Alexis Salfatte (alexis_salfatte@hotmail.com, send an e-mail before you call his cell phone). Usually he shows part of a movie and a teacher makes comments about the movie, leading a discussion. This evening is free of charge (if you want to bring your own food) or there is a small charge for the pizza or sandwich and beverage that Alexis serves. You can meet other students, you can ask questions about this confusing culture called "the USA" and you can take more steps to find a successful life in the USA. Please call ahead to confirm that you want to attend—and to reserve a slice of pizza or a sandwich. :)

If this information is not accurate, you can find the new address at "Culture Night" on www.teacherstoteachers.com.

A NOTE TO THE TEACHER
(Students can read this, too)

This book is a combination of:
a) Textbook for a class to read together.
b) Workbook for a class to work together.

c) Advice book (for a class to discuss and use).

The structure of each chapter is simple:
There are readings.
There are exercises (questions, compositions, fill-in-the-blanks).
There are photos.
There are e-mail addresses (write to the people in these pages and on the web pages at www.geocities.com/novanewspaper/page1.html).

Advice is the focus here. We want new students to learn from experienced students.

You don't need to start at Chapter One and work through the book in the order of the chapters. Let the students jump around, following their interests.

Your role as the facilitator of the class is to ask each student to find a partner. The partners work together to read and understand the readings, to complete the exercises and to find the answers.

We hope that students can be independent. Your job is to push them to work in pairs and to talk about the things they read about.

The teacher can also bring in articles, photos and videos to support the topics. The objective is to help students anticipate problems and learn techniques to succeed in the USA.

The standard signals in the book are the following phrases: EXERCISE, READING, ADVICE, PHOTO, and HOMEWORK.

EXERCISE: work with your partner.
READING: read together or each student reads one sentence.
ADVICE: Divide students into groups of two. Ask student A to give the advice to the partner, Student B.

IAGI = It's a good idea…For example, IAGI to go for a walk after dinner to help your digestion.

PHOTO: look at the photo and describe the activity. Example: "He is eating a sandwich. It looks delicious. Perhaps it is a chicken salad sandwich."

HOMEWORK: In addition to the suggestions in this book, go into www.teacherstoteachers.com to find more homework.

Each section is given a number, like "1.5 Advice." You can tell the students, "For homework, read sections 1.1 and 1.4 and do the exercise in 1.3. The composition in 1.6 is optional." (Write the numbers on the board to help the students, or-better-ask a student to write what you said on the board.

The teacher needs to encourage students to talk to each other. These exercises are designed to give you opportunities to talk and write. To help the teacher, we ask students to read ahead of the class and think about writing three or four sentences each day before class…just to warm up your brain!

If this book looks like a bunch of articles that were thrown together, you are right. It is a project compiled by students in November and December 2000. There is a lot of advice here. We hope you will send us more advice so we can put it in the web site.

EXERCISE (work with a partner)
What is annoying to U.S. listeners? Find a synonym (work with your partner and have a conversation) for "annoying."

A. It is annoying to me when visitors don't say the last letter in a word.
EXAMPLE: Plea spea lou er an say ii agai
CORRECT: Please speak louder and say it again.

Synonym for annoying…
It is annoying when a visitor says: _____
It is bothersome when…
It is disturbing when…
It is irritating when…
It is upsetting when…

I am annoyed by visitors who say:
It is bothersome by…
It is disturbing by…
It is irritating by…
It is upsetting when…

It annoys me when a visitor says: "He eat many bananas yesterday."
It bothers me when…
It disturbs me when…
It irritates me when…
It upsets me when…

It grates me when…
It rubs me the wrong way when…

B. THESE ARE ANNOYING SENTENCES
1 Please explain me.

2 Please tell to me something.

3 Please say me what I need to do.

4 I has three brother and two sister.

5 He have two cars.

6 She has two houses diferents.
(Word order, the adjective does not need the "s".)

7 What did he found in the classroom?

8 What did he saw yesterday?

9 He didn't found the car key.

10 He didn't found the cars key. OR He didn't found the cars' key.

CORRECTED FORM
1 Please explain to me.
2 Please tell me something.
3 Please say to me what I need to do.
4 I have three brothers and two sisters (say the last letter clearly).
5 He has two cars.
6 She has two different houses.
7 What did he find in the classroom?

8 What did he see yesterday?
9 He didn't find the car key.
10 He didn't find the car's key. (Put the apostrophe in the right place)

C. Make your story short. I'm really annoyed when the visitor explains everything to me.
EXAMPLE: AV = annoying visitor
"When did you arrive in the USA?"
AV: I think it was 3 months ago…no, it was on July 14…oh, wait a minute, it was after the big parade…Oh, yes, I came in Miami and it was raining, so it was in August, and now it is December so it was four months ago.

BETTER: NV = nice visitor
"When did you arrive in the USA?"
NV: About three months ago.

Most U.S. people speak in approximate language. They use words like "about" and "approximately." Just give an answer. You don't need to be exact.

If an exact answer is needed, the person will ask another question, "When exactly did you arrive?"
NV: Well, let me see. Give me a moment to think. Excuse me, so much has happened that I can't remember exactly…oh, yes it was on August 1.

The visitor is "buying time" and filling the pause. Most U.S. listeners are not comfortable with empty space or quiet time. Many people from Asia are comfortable with "silence" during a conversation. When you are with a U.S. person, say something, say it quickly, then ask a question back. It's like a game of ping-pong, tennis and volleyball. You need to send the conversation or the ball back to the other person. For more information, see www.geocities.com/talkinternational/conversation.html

D. The Structure of Each Chapter

If you do everything in this book, you will practice writing, reading, listening and speaking. Here are some of the sections found in each chapter:

READING

A composition by an ESL student starts each chapter. It is an actual composition with errors. You need to find the errors with your partner. A corrected composition appears later in the chapter, usually three pages after the beginning of the chapter.

ABBREVIATIONS: What is NASA? What does the abbreviation stand for?

ADVICE: "It's a good idea to…"

INTERNET: "Here are some internet sites for you to visit to find more information."

(If you know about other web sites, please send a message to english-lesson@mail.com and we will consider adding your suggestion to our web site.) This section includes advice about where you can subscribe to an internet e-letter and receive a new vocabulary lesson each week. Here's another example: When you need a doctor's advice, go to www.medicine.com/ or www.md.com/. EXERCISE: visit this web site and ask a question (search for an answer). Print the page, bring the answer to class and pin it to the class notice board.

Your classroom needs a notice board or bulletin board or a corkboard. Ask the teacher to create a space where students can bring interesting articles and print-outs from the Internet.

LETTER: "Write a letter to the manager of the store to explain your problem. Ask for something." You can also write a letter or an e-mail message to one of the authors of this book.

LISTENING: "Listen to suggestions from students who had a similar problem." You can listen to a conversation on the CD-rom called "CD-1" (available from www.teacherstoteachers.com).

GRAMMAR: Fill in the blank: He is a _____ man. He is a s_____. He wants to s_____ (succeed, success, successful).

VOCABULARY: Give two synonyms for "garbage." Write the opposite. (What IS the opposite??? "valuable stuff"??? trash, waste…things I want to keep).

WRITE A DIALOG: You have a neighbor from another country. Juana and Ramon Martinez have a son Jorge who is always getting into trouble. Ramon is a truck driver, so he is out of town at least five nights each week. Juana doesn't speak English very well, so she often comes looking for your help.

There is another neighbor, the Smiths. John and Mary Smith have been married 25 years. She is a real estate broker and John is a teacher in the local high school. Ralph is the teenage son (he is 17) and Gertrude is the daughter (she is 20 years old and she attends the local university).

Write the dialog with your partner. You can be on the telephone or you can talk directly to the people. You must decide whom you are talking to. Example: Jorge broke the window of your house with a baseball. By telephone…
You: Hello, Mr. Martinez.
Ramon: Yes?

Y: This is your neighbor. I'm sorry to bother you.
R: No problem. How can I help you?
Y: Well, I have your son's baseball. It broke my window.
R: Oh, no. what window did it break?
Y: The one next to the garage.
R: How much will it cost?
Y: About fifty dollars for the glass.
R: I'll come over to see it.
(etc.)

Now you are ready to start this book. Let's begin with a look at your goals and "success."

What is "Success"?

This section begins with some exercises that will build a feeling of success and accomplishment. Good luck and enjoy the work!

0.1
The first exercise: The Map (PAIRWORK)
DIRECTIONS: Get a local map and work with a partner to find these interesting points. (You can find good maps on www.sunny.org and www.miami.com.)
Point to three shopping centers (shopping malls).
For students in South Florida, find the following: Bayside, Cocowalk, Aventura, the Falls, Sawgrass Mills Mall, Galleria, Broward, Festival, the Swap Shop, East Las Olas, Boca Town Center, Palm Beach Gardens Mall, Mizner Center.
Where is a good place to spend an afternoon?
Tell me about a nice restaurant near your home in Florida.
Where is a good beach?
Can you recommend a good movie theater?
What supermarket do you recommend?
Can you suggest a good pharmacy near your home?

OPTIONAL
Find three museums.
Find the Miami Seaquarium.
Find all of the Piers in Broward County.

0.2
Who is in my class?
DIRECTIONS: Collect this information

1. Introduce yourself to your classmates: First name, e-mail address, hobbies, profession, dreams.

2. What is the phone number of the teacher?

3. What is the phone number of the school?

4. What are the phone numbers of your classmates? (You can call them once a week to check their pronunciation and to practice speaking over the phone.)

5. If you are late, what number do you need to call? What are the rules of the classroom? (Is it okay to walk in quietly if you are 30 minutes late?)

6. In your school in your country, was it possible to enter a class after the lesson started? Could you be 20 minutes late?

7. If the teacher is late, what will you do? (Do you have the mobile phone number of the teacher? Is there a book called "Five-Minute Activities" in the classroom?)

0.3
Communicate with another class
DIRECTIONS: Introduce yourself and your classmates to other classes. Take a photo (You can use a Polaroid camera or a digital camera to make the photos):
a) put the photo on paper;

b) write your names and professions and your hometowns on the photo;

c) Send the photo to another class or another school;

d) Make copies for each person in the class.

Make a web site or write short introductions and your e-mail address. Send the page to another class (fax 954-565-8718 is the number at TALK School of Languages. 954 262-3913 is the Fax at Nova's English School).

Write a letter to another class.

For example, look at the web page at these locations:

www.geocities.com/novanewspaper/page1.html and

www.geocities.com/stevemccrea/photos00-10.html

www.teacherstoteachers.com (click on "PHOTOS NOVA TALK").

You can write to the e-mail addresses of the people who are listed on these pages.

NOTE to the Teacher or the curious students: To make a web site, go to www.geocities.com/countries2001/insturction.html and you will find two pages of step-by-step instructions for your class.

0.4

What is "success"?

PAIR WORK (CONVERSATION)

With your partner, take five minutes and write an answer to this question.

1. Is money part of "success"?

2. Is a fast car part of "success"?

3. Is a family part of "success"?

4. What is part of "success"?

After you have written the answers to these questions, read the next sentences: Are you isolated? Are you confused? Do you feel alone? You are not alone. You can write to other students who were new to the USA and who used to be nervous about the future.

Here is a Letter to New Students from Steve (Editor of this book), englishlesson@mail.com:

Hi,
I'm a teacher of English to Adults. My class and I have decided to pull together a book about English as a Second Language for people who want to live in the USA. Some books will teach you "How to Survive in English" or "Basic English for Survival in a new country." We want to make a book to help you succeed.

Success means many things to many people. Many people come to the USA and they see:
-large houses.
-fast cars.
-wonderful jobs in beautiful office buildings.
-women in beautiful clothes.
-men in motor boats.
-children on expensive bicycles and with Nike shoes.

I asked my students, "What is success?" and this is what they wrote.

I consider myself a successful person. I have all the things that I need. I am a healthy person. I have the chance to go to university and study to be a more educated person. I found the most beautiful friends in the whole world My family and friends love me a lot.

Success is something that we can get through many ways and many subjects. You can be successful in our family, in your job, in your studies, etc.

You can get success in a project or in a little goal. The most important thing in life isn't to have success. It's to look for the success.

(The journey is more important than the goal.)

If you are successful in some topic, you have to tell other people how you achieved it so that people can have success, too.

Success for me is to be in peace with myself, doing things to improve, to grow with my family, to make an effort to be a better person each day, to help other people to be successful, to be healthy, to speak English and to have a happy and connected family.

Success is any goal that you want.
Success is anything that you get with a good goal.
Success includes connection to the community and to other people.

I understand what my students wrote. They know that we can have large houses, fast cars, terrific jobs, beautiful clothes, motor boats, expensive bicycles and Nike shoes, but we might not feel successful.

Without family, love, friends and health, we are not really successful. We can be successful on a material level. We can have a lot of physical things, but we have a feeling: "something is not here." A voice in our heads tells us, "Something is missing."

This book is about our success in becoming connected with our new community. I know that when I first moved to Florida, I did not feel connected to my new city. I could drive around and I knew where to find the beach, good stores, the center of the city and the safer areas of the city. I didn't feel successful because I didn't feel connected to my family (they were 1600 km away), I had lost my girlfriend and I didn't know the joy of being part of a community. I felt isolated. It took several years (after I met my wife) before I came to feel connected to this city.

This book will point you toward your happiness and success. We want to show you how to become connected, how to break the isolation, and how to feel "comfortable in my new home."

0.5
LET'S BREAK THE ISOLATION.
Step one: Get an e-mail address.
Step two: Send your e-mail address to englishlesson@mail.com (tell me "one lesson once a month" or "three lessons each week" and I'll put you on my e-mail list of students who want to receive lesions via e-mail.). Ask for an e-mail partner or ask a question ("I'm new to Miami. Can you tell me where I can find._____?").
Step three: Read the dozens of e-mail letters that my students will send to you.
Step four: Do something. Join a group. Visit a language school and ask to sit in a class for two hours (one hour in grammar, one hour in conversation). Join a group of students for lunch after the class. Talk with someone from another country.
Step five: Do something again. Smile. Breathe. Look at the lists of suggestions in this book. Visit "It's a good idea" www.angelfire.com/fl4/good-idea.html and see some of the good ideas that my students wrote. Connect yourself to the community.
Step six: Keep doing something until you are successful.

               *   *   *

Step two hundred forty-seven: Share your time, your advice and your love with another visitor. Help a new person and you'll feel even more connected.

Thank you,
Steve, englishlesson@mail.com

Many, many thanks to the dozens of other students who helped with this project (and the thousands of other students who continue to contribute to make this a fun and useful book for isolated people).

0.6
More definitions of success…
I consider myself a successful person. I have all the things that I need. I am a healthy person, I have a wonderful and a united family. I have the chance to go to university and study to be a more educated person. I found the most beautiful friends in the whole world My family and friend love me a lot. I know what I want to get in life and I work to obtain it. I have the support and the understanding of all the persons that I love. I'm very happy and that's the principal reason why I know that I have success. Nothing else matters if you are unhappy. We have to live each day like it's going to be the last day and we have to be grateful.

Success is something that we can get through many ways and many subjects. You can be successful in our family, in your job, in your studies, etc. You can get success sin a project or in a little goal. The most important thing in life isn't to have success it's to look for the success.

(There is an ancient philosophy that says: The journey is more important than the goal.)

The fact of being successful doesn't mean that you don't talk or help other people. If you are successful in some topic, you have to tell other people how you achieved it so that people can have success, too.

Success for me is to be in peace with myself, doing things to improve, to grow with my family. There are several points that are important to be a successful person: interior peace, some money, professional development, making your own effort to be a better person each day and helping the people who are next to you to be successful people, to be healthy, to speak English and to have a successful family.

Failure is all the things that you can't get for your internal satisfaction.

Success is any goal that you want.

(I agree! Success is having goals. We complete some goals and we make new ones.—Steve)

Success is anything that you get with a good goal. Failure is something that you do and the result is bad.

I feel successful when I can help a person solve a problem. I like to recommend a good teacher or a good doctor, I like to recommend a good mechanic or a good restaurant. I want the new person to feel connected to the community.

For me, it is a success to get my family united. It is very important to feel good with myself. Also I am very happy if my children go the correct way. My husband and I are working very hard for that, but not only my children. I'm also successful if my husband and I find the correct job. We think in the measure that you feel good, you will obtain whatever you want.

0.7
PAIR WORK (CONVERSATION)
Look at the answer that you and your partner wrote at the beginning of this lesson. Do you want to add something to your answer?

0.8

LETTER

Please write to one of the people in the front of the book and describe your definition of success.

0.9

The Next Exercise: Class Rules

Work with your partner to create a list of rules for the class to follow. Consider the following points:

Class starts at _____. When is a student called "late"?

What is your opinion of beepers and cell phones (also called "handies")?

Can coffee be brought into the classrooms?

When you are finished with your list of rules for the classroom, compare your list with the list from other students.

0.10

The Next Exercise: Phone numbers from your classmates

Your classmates are going to be your fellow teachers. Each of you will help each other.

"Get the Telephone Number" is an exercise in listening. You try to get the phone number of at least 80% of your class.

a) Ask for the phone number of two or three classmates.

b) When you go home, call these classmates. Ask for phone numbers of other classmates.

c) Call the new phone numbers and try to find numbers of other classmates.

d) At the end of the exercise you might have a full list of the class' phone numbers.

What is the latest time in the evening (and on weekends) that you can call?

Discuss your homework with your partner and with other students.

At least once each week, call a student on the phone list and talk for three minutes. Ask, "Is this a good time to practice conversation with you?" or "Hi, did you finish the homework? Do you want to check the answers with me?"

If it is not a good time, then you need to arrange another time. Remember, it's good practice for both the speaker and the listener, the caller and the receiver of the phone call.

0.11
Methods of Learning
PAIRWORK: Work with your partner to answer these questions:
How do you learn? Do you prefer to listen to a new word? Do you prefer to see a new word in writing? Do you prefer to see a word in action? Do you like it when your teacher is very active? Do you want to touch "a dog" or see a picture of "dog" or see the word "dog" on the white board or do you want the teacher to repeat "dog" (so you understand the pronunciation)? Do you want your teacher to check your pronunciation?

The methods of learning are:
1) I See
2) I Hear
3) I Do
Note to the Instructor: Ask pairs of the students to teach a grammar or vocabulary lesson to the rest of the class. Ask them to teach the same material in three ways, to help all types of students to learn the material.

The methods of learning create the "Methods of Teaching" (see also Chapter 12 about Teaching Techniques).

The principle method used by TALK Teachers at Nova's English Language Program is "What is good for the student?" In general, we put the student in the center and we ask the student to produce. We want you to direct the class. Tell us what you want to study.

The instructors have a plan. We can add to the plan if the students say, "I want to practice more conversations" or "I want to prepare for a job interview" or "What do I say when I am looking for something at Home Depot?"

We use a lot of pairwork. We often ask the students to choose a topic in a book. Perhaps it is grammar, perhaps the lesson is a group of related vocabulary words. We ask you, the student, to work together with your partner to make a lesson.

For example, you can make a little test using IN or ON. Create a lesson with exercises and blanks. If you want to test another student's ability to learn "in" or "on", you can make sentences like these:
The cat is _____ the television.
The mouse is _____ the cat. (:))
The pencil is _____ the table.
A pen is _____ the right drawer.

Let's move now to the main categories (there are 11 of them) of Life in the USA. You can study any category first.

Part A: The Big Categories

The previous page explains the structure of each chapter. At the end of each chapter is a list of "recommendations." We'd like to start with a few stories about "the first things I noticed when I arrived in the USA."

1. Finance

There are photos for this chapter at *www.teacherstoteachers.com*, then click on "ESL BOOK" and click on "Chapter 1."

1.1
READING
The first time I came to the USA…. (Please correct the parts that are underlined.)

1-Gas Station
It was the first time that I was going to fill up. I was alone in my cousin's car and I didn't have petrol. I went into a gas station, I parked beside one of the gas machines and I stayed in the car waiting for the gas-pump or attendant. When I looked around to other people…..I saw that they were filling up by themselves, and I already had 5 minutes stopped, waiting for someone!

Here, in the USA, there are no attendants in the gas stations, you have to do it by yourself. Before you fill up, you have to go into the little shop (those that usually are in the gas stations) to pay. They active the machine where you are, so you can fill up. Or you can get a little piece called "speed pas". You buy that piece, and every time you'll go to fill up, you present the piece on the sign with the red horse that says "speed pass", and they charge it to your credit card.

2-Seven Eleven

I was surprised when I went to this place for first time with my father. It's like a little supermarket and bakery, where you can take a sandwich, or a pastry, and you can serve you a coffee by yourself….and the most amazing is that you can eat and drink whatever you want inside the shop, and when you go to the till, you tell the cashier what did you eat and drink….and you pay.

For me, it's amazing because I come from Venezuela, and I'm sure that in my country, it can't never exist a shop like this one. Everybody would lie in the till, and it would be a chaos……it's another culture and way to think.

Daniela Patruno danibabe81@hotmail.com

1.2

PAIRWORK

1. With your partner, answer these questions: What did Daniela notice? What was different in the USA? What is wrong with the words that are underlined in the story above?

2. Tell your partner about something unusual that you noticed when you arrived in the USA.

3. Think about life in your country and life in the USA. What is different in your country compared to the USA?

Corrections

1-Seven Eleven

It was the first time that I was going to fill up. I was alone in my cousin's car and I didn't have petrol (gasoline). I went into a gas station, I parked beside one of the gas machines and I stayed in the car waiting for the gas-attendant. When I looked around to other people…..I saw that they were filling up by themselves, and I already had stopped for 5 minutes, waiting for someone!

Here, in the USA, there are no attendants in the gas stations. You have to do it by yourself. Before you fill up, you have to go into the little shop (those that usually are in the gas stations) to pay. They activate the machine where you are, so you can fill up. Or you can get a little piece called "speed pass." You buy that piece, and every time you'll go to fill up, you present the piece on the sign with the red horse that says "speed pass", and they charge it to your credit card.

These sentences are more natural: I didn't have gasoline. I stayed in the car waiting for the gas-pump attendant. I had already stopped for five minutes., waiting for someone. There are no attendants in the gas stations. You have to do the pumping by yourself. They activate the machine (they turn on the machine). Pass has two "s"s.

2-Seven Eleven
I was surprised when I went to this place for first time with my father. It's like a little supermarket and bakery, where you can take a sandwich, or a pastry, and you can serve you a coffee by yourself….and the most amazing is that you can eat and drink whatever you want inside the shop, and when you go to the till, you tell the cashier what did you eat and drink….and you pay.

For me, it's amazing because I come from Venezuela, and I'm sure that in my country, there can't ever exist a shop like this one. Everybody would lie in the till, and it would be a chaos……it's another culture and way to think.

Another way: in my country it's impossible to find a shop like this one.
Answers
These sentences are more natural:
You can serve yourself a cup of coffee.
The most amazing thing is that you can eat and drink…. (use "thing")
You tell the cashier what you ate and drank.
In my country, a shop like this can't ever exist.

In my country, it's impossible to find a shop like this one.
It would be chaos.

1.3
PAIR WORK (CONVERSATION)
Here are some words that you need to know. Work with your partner
and write a sentence with each word or phrase:
Mortgage for the house
Car loan
Student Loan
Credit card
Interest
Interest rate
The rate of interest
Principal
Payment
Mother's maiden name
Show your sentences to another pair of students. Your teacher will also
check your answers.

1.4
PAIRWORK
Work with your partner and answer these questions.

How do people get money from a bank in your country?
Do you have questions about the banking system in the USA?
What surprised you when you came to the USA about money? About
banks?
What is the interest rate in your country for a house mortgage?
Describe a problem that you had in the USA.
What did you do?
Do you have any recommendations?

1.5
Look for the errors
READING and DISCUSSION
Talk with your partner about these responses by ESL students:
How do people get money from a bank in your country?
People get money from a savings and a checking account, or by a loan for a car or a home.

Do you have questions about the banking system in the USA?
-When was the banking system in the USA created?
-What do I need here to have a credit line from the bank?
-How many kinds of accounts are here?
-How do people can get a loan from a bank?
-How can I open an account being immigrant?

What surprised you when you came to the USA about money? About banks?
-The money in USA is a valuable thing.
-The transactions by phone.
-The banks are empty and you don't lose much time to visit them.
-The people use cash. In my country the people use more checks.
-The money here is a valuable thing.
-The interest you get when you open a saving account.

What is the interest rate in your country for a house mortgage?
The interest rate for a house loan (mortgage) in the Dominican Republic is about 23% per year.
-About 28% (Venezuela)
-25% per year. (Venezuela)
-Between 10% and 12%
-About 25% by year (Colombia)
-In the USA in 2000, the rate is less than 10%.

Describe a problem that you had in the USA.
It took me a long time (almost a year) to get a credit record. (a credit history).

What did you do?
I got a credit card by a deposit of money in a bank and then I proved that I was solvent.

Here is another student's replies:

How do people get money from a bank in your country?
-When you have an account in the bank, with a guarantor, with a good life curriculum.
-Fill an application form and attach some copies that show who are you, what do you have…etc. Or you can charge a check.

Describe a problem that you had in the USA. What did you do?
-When I came to the USA, it took me a long time to get a credit record. I got a credit card by a deposit of money in a bank and then I proved to be solvent.

If you want to read the replies of other students, go to www.geocities.com/talkinternational/finance.html

Do you have any recommendations?
I think that when we pay for rent, we must have a check in the credit bureau. It is a good idea to have a positive credit history.

Don't forget to request a new set of checks when you begin to use the last twenty checks.

1.6
ABBREVIATIONS:
What is ATM? What does the abbreviation stand for?
FDIC
Fannie Mae
IRS
ID
SSN
GNP
DJIA
S&P
NYSE
NASDAQ
IPO
YTD   (for   the   answers,   check   the   web   site   at www.teacherstoteachers.com)

1.7
ADVICE
It's a good idea to…" IAGI
It's a good idea to get more information about a charity before you donate money to it. You can call the Florida Division of Consumer Services at 1-800-435-7352. Ask for a report about the charity's past record of administration. How much money do they spend to raise money? If they raise $500,000 and they spend $250,000 to raise the money, their administrative cost is 50% of the total. (This is not good!)

Freedom from Hunger www.freefromhunger.com is a charity in Davis, California. It is registered in the State of Florida. 1-800 708-2555 is their toll-free number.

1.8

Ask Steve

"What's your favorite credit card and frequent-flyer program?"

I like the Visa card that is connected to Southwest Airlines. You get a free ticket every 16,000 dollars (most other cards give a ticket in the USA for $25,000 of spending). I like Southwest because the airline lets you fly on any flight. Other airlines limit the number of frequent-flyer seats on each plane. If there is a space on Southwest and you have a "Free Ticket" coupon, you can fly! It's a great airline (the employees are owners) and the employees are very friendly. 1-800-I-FLY-SWA. (What are the numbers?) See the Answer at the end of the chapter. To apply for the card, call 1-800-450-8290 or go to the Southwest web site and ask for the current VISA card bank…www.southwest.com.

How can I get a Social Security Number (SSN)?

It's a good idea to get a Tax Payer ID (identification number) from the IRS. The Social Security Number is given to citizens and residents. The Taxpayer ID is for financial matters and you can use it to open a bank account. (The IRS wants to know who you are if your account earns interest, so they can tax you!). However, you usually need to be a resident with a work permit to get an SSN.

1.9

INTERNET

"Here are some internet sites for you to visit to find more information."

(If you know about other web sites, please send a message to english-lesson@mail.com and we will consider adding your suggestion to our web site.)

www.bankofamerica.com/

The Bank of America web site is full of useful information.

On the Web: www.geocities.com/talkinternational/finance.html

1.10
LETTER
"Write a letter to the manager of the bank to explain a problem. Ask for something. Ask for help."

1.11
LISTENING
"Listen to suggestions from students who had a similar problem."
On the CD-1, available from www.teacherstoteachers.com, you can listen to the conversation. With your partner, listen to ten sentences, write down the entire sentences and then show the sentences to your teacher.

1.12
GRAMMAR
Fill in the blank: He is a s_____ man. He is a s_____. He wants to s_____ (succeed, success, successful).

I went to the law office and I gave a _____ (I told a lawyer about the car crash that I saw).
I want to make a _____ into my bank account.
Where is the place to buy things for the office? Go to Office _____ (deposit, depot, deposition)

1.13
VOCABULARY
Give two synonyms for "garbage." Write the opposite. (What is the opposite of "valuable stuff"??? trash, waste…things I want to keep)

1.14
READING
Subscribe to an internet e-letter and receive a new vocabulary lesson each week.
Motivational Quotes of the Day for October 23, 2000
Be faithful to that which exists nowhere but in yourself-and thus make yourself indispensable.—Andre Gide

Young people have an almost biological destiny to be hopeful.—Marshall Ganz, quoted by Sara Rimer in New York Times

They can conquer who believe they can.—Virgil

Success in business requires training and discipline and hard work. But if you're not frightened by these things, the opportunities are just as great today as they ever were.—David Rockefeller

For more quotes, visit The Quotations Page, www.quotationspage.com.

1.15
JOKES
These words come from Will Rogers, a humorist and a philosopher who died in 1935.
Ask your partner about the words you don't understand. If you both don't understand a word, underline it and ask your teacher to explain it to you.

1 Don't squat with your spurs on.
2 Lettin' the cat outta the bag is a whole lot easier 'n puttin' it back in.
3 If you're ridin' ahead of the herd, take a look back every now and then to make sure it's still there.
4 If you get to thinkin' you're a person of some influence, try orderin' somebody else's dog around.
5 If you find yourself in a hole, the first thing to do is stop diggin'.
6 The quickest way to double your money is to fold it over and put it back in your pocket.
7 Never miss a good chance to shut up.
8 There are three kinds of men. The one that learns by reading. The few who learn by observation. The rest of them have to pee on the electric fence for themselves.

1.16
WRITE A DIALOG
Part A: Choose one of these situations and imagine the words that are said. Work with your partner.
Part B: Create another situation. Describe the situation and (if you want to) send it by e-mail to englishlesson@mail.com.

Situations: Finance
a. You are at the bank and you notice smoke coming from the safe deposit room. Soon smoke has filled the entire bank. An alarm starts to ring. The door to the room is very hot. Should you open the door? Use words like "close to the ground" and "a wet cloth".
b. Jorge comes to you and says, "I have $400 and I want to open a bank account. My mother is too scared to go to the bank with me. Can you come with us?"
c. You found a lost wallet. Don't mail it to the address on the driver license. First you need to call and then arrange to return it.
d. Jorge lost his wallet. He wants your help in finding it.

Situation # 1 (Finance)

Daniela wants to buy a car here, but somebody told her that she has to negotiate the prices with the dealer. Which are the most common phrases to do it? Which are some prices for different kinds of cars here? Do I have to ask for a guarantee? How long do I ask for the guarantee? (How long should the guarantee be?)

ANSWER. 1-800-I-FLY-SWA. What are the numbers? 1-800-435-9792

2. Health

There are photos for this chapter at *www.teacherstoteachers.com*, then click on "ESL BOOK" and click on "Chapter 2."

2.1
READING
Find the errors. The answers are at the end of the chapter.
"The medical service is something that cannot be fair. It has to be excellent."
In Venezuela, there are so many health problems, overcoat in the rural zones of the country, due to the bad quality that the public hospitals have. Really, the problem is economic. Those hospitals are subsidized by the government, or should be subsidized by it, but they don't pay the doctors, and the hospitals don't have any founds to buy the necessary materials and instruments, so the attention to the patients is very bad, and that causes many epidemical diseases in the rural population. I'm going to talk about one specific disease: The Ancylostomiasis. That's an intestinal disease caused by one parasite that the rural people catch thru the faeces in the soil. That disease is very serious, because the parasite develops into the person, it grows, and causes many problems, like anemia, weakness, and also death in some cases. People cannot go to any hospitals to receive treatment, because they are bad attended because the shortage of materials, or simply there are no doctors who work without charge.
The MSAS (Ministerio de Sanidad y Asistencia Social) have completed a lot of studies to know the number of people with each disease and

those numbers have increased notably in the last 20 years, due to the public health problem in the country.

2.2
PAIR WORK (CONVERSATION)
Here are some words that you need to know. Work with your partner and write a sentence with each word or phrase:
Doctors
Dentists
Checkup
Appointment
Co-payment
Ailment
Illness
Serious condition
Health Care Programs (HMOs, PPOs, etc.)

2.3
PAIRWORK
Work with your partner and answer these questions.

Do you have questions about the medical system in the USA?
What surprised you when you came to the USA about the doctors here?
Describe a problem that you had in the USA.
What did you do?
Do you have any recommendations?

2.4
READING and DISCUSSION
Talk with your partner about these responses by ESL students:

Do you have questions about the medical system in the USA?
Where can I consult for an apoiment with a specific doctor?
(it is "appointment"….not "apoiment")
Do you have a kind of federation to control the system?
Do you have public hospitals? How is their quality?
Why the doctors don't take enough time with the patients?
What does "medicare" means?
How many health insurance companies are there in the USA?
How do you find a doctor or a dentist?

What surprised you when you came to the USA about the doctors here?
They are expensive, and more even to the foreign people.
(it is "even more"…….not "more even")
If you don't have insurance, it's very difficult to get attention.
Doctors attend patients very quickly.
The doctors don't have enough personal contact with their patients.
(Said by a doctor)

Describe a problem that you had in the USA. Why did you do?
Last year I went to a dentist here, and he charged me $70. I had to pay but I won't go to a dentist here, again.
I had to wait six hours in a public hospital with my son sick. My child had high fever and they didn't do anything. I had to go to a private doctor….They recieve my child and gave me the prescription.
(it is "my sick son" and "received"………not "my son sick" and "recieve")
I didn't have any insurance, and I tried to get one, thru the company that I works for.
(it is "I work"………not "I works")

Do you have any recommendations?
Try to go to the doctors in your country, when you'll stay on vacation. If you are American citizen, the only thing that you can do, is to prevent

diseases, don't get wet, wash the vegetables, etc. Anyway, the doctors are not as expensive to you as to us.

Make an appoiment, and to be punctual in your date and hour.

(it is "appointment"..........not "appoinment")

2.5

ABBREVIATIONS

On a piece of paper write the words for these abbreviations. Work with your partner.

What is MD? What does the abbreviation stand for?

HMO

COBRA

OSHA

PPO

RN

DDS

The answers are at the end of the chapter.

2.6

ADVICE

"It's a good idea to…" IAGI…

IAGI to check your water. You need to check for parasites in your tap water. Cryptosporidium is in some water and you need to check your water for this parasite.

For details about your water, visit www.epa.gov/safewater or call 1-800-426-4791.

IAGI to avoid breathing the air near mouse droppings. Hanta virus is carried in the urine of mice and there is a strong presence of the Hanta virus in the Southwest of the USA. (When I first heard about this, I wondered "Why has nobody told me about this?" "Why didn't some-body tell me about the Hanta virus?")

From www.drkoop.com
"Hanta virus is carried by rodents, particularly deer mice, and is present in their urine and feces. The Hanta virus does not cause disease in the carrier animal but it does in man. Humans are thought to become infected when they are exposed to contaminated dust from the nests or droppings of mice. The disease is not, however, passed between humans. Contaminated dust is often encountered when cleaning long-vacated dwellings, sheds, or other enclosed areas."
www.drkoop.com/conditions/ency/article/001382.htm

Shaking hands and touching door handles are the two surest ways to get cold germs. IAGI to wash your hands carefully at least once every two hours. A surgeon, Tony P., suggested to me that a good way to clean under the fingernails is to use a small brush with plastic bristles (hairs).

2.7
INTERNET
"Here are some internet sites for you to visit to find more information."
(If you know about other web sites, please send a message to english-lesson@mail.com and we will consider adding your suggestion to our web site.) Subscribe to an internet e-letter and receive a new vocabulary lesson each week.

Family.com: Skills: The Parent Problem Solver
Do you have questions about your child's behavior and development? Are you looking for the best parenting techniques? Whether you're struggling with a tempestuous toddler or a pimple-prone preteen, we'll help you find the answers you need. Go to www.family.com

When you need a doctor's advice, go to www.medicine.com/ or www.md.com/. EXERCISE: visit this web site and ask a question (search for an answer). Print the page, bring the answer to class and pin it to the class notice board.

www.broward.org/medical.htm
Click on "Health Guide for the Medically Perplexed" (perplexed = confused).

www.broward.org/spi00200.htm
EXERCISE: call one of the phone numbers on this page and ask to speak with one of the information officers. Ask a question about medicine, health or safety.

On the Web: www.geocities.com/talkinternational/health.html
Very important advice about canned drinks (sodas and beer).

www.realage.com then click on the topic that you want to learn about (for example, "colds and flu")

2.8
LETTER
"Write a letter to a doctor to describe a problem. Ask for something."
Then show the letter to your teacher.

2.9
LISTENING
On the CD-1, available from www.teacherstoteachers.com, you can listen to the conversation. With your partner, listen to ten sentences, write down the entire sentences and then show the sentences to your teacher.

2.10
GRAMMAR
Put these words in the sentences
sees, seas
he _____ a shark in the seven _____.

in, on
Children are playing _____ the road
There is a mouse _____ the table.

rowed, rode, road, row
The _____ is narrow
She _____ the bus.
She _____ the boat.
In London, the people argued about the soccer game. There was a
big"_____"
(It sounds like "now")

sight, site, side, sighed
The web _____ is ready.
Please walk on the _____ of the road.
He had a headache, so he _____/
The _____ is beautiful.. I love the view from this place.

2.11
JOKE
Q: Do you know what it means to come home to a man who'll give
you
love, affection, tenderness and understanding?
A: It means you're in the wrong house.
~~~~~~

The son came home from school and said to his father, "Today I learned that in some parts of Africa, the man doesn't know his wife until he marries her.

The dad replied, "That happens in most countries, son."

~~~~~~

A mother was reading a book about animals to her 3-year-old daughter.

The mother said, "What does the cow say?"

The child answered, "Moo!"

The mother then said, "Great! What does the cat say?"

The child replied, "Meow."

The mother exclaimed, "Oh, you're so smart! What does the frog say?"

The wide-eyed little 3-year-old looked up at her mother and in her deepest voice replied, "Bud."

2.12

VOCABULARY

Draw a human body. Write the names of at least 20 parts of the body. What is the wrist, fist, waist, ankle, uncle, waste, thigh, shin, chin, brow, and cheek? Work with your partner.

When you are finished with your drawing, write five sentences in the past using bleed, break, bruise, scrape, cut, heal and scar.

Examples:

I _____ my finger last year. It _____ quickly. Now I have a _____.

(Use these words: scar, cut, heal)

My sister b_____ her leg last year.

(Use this word: break)

Last night I bumped my arm against the wall. I br_____ my muscle.

(Use this word: bruise)

Now write your own sentences.

OPTION

Create sentences and remove one word. Give three options for the word (similar to the example). Then give your sentences to another group and see if they can find the answer.

I cut my foot. Now it is _____ (blood, bleeding, bloody, bled).

If this is difficult for you, ask your teacher to review "Emergency Room English" (the language and vocabulary that you need when you go to the hospital!).

2.13

WORKSHEET

Idioms, Proverbs, Phrasal verbs

1. The best things in life are _____ (tree, free, see, green)

2. It's nice to walk on the _____ side of the street (sun sunny mirror)

3. It's _____ loud in this room. (two to too)

2.14

WRITE A DIALOG

Part A: Choose one of these situations and imagine the words that are said. Work with your partner.

Part B: Create another situation. Describe the situation and (if you want to) send it by e-mail to englishlesson@mail.com.

Health

a. You meet Mr. Martinez (Carlos) at the hospital. He is your son's math teacher. Start a conversation.

b. You meet Mr. Smith, your neighbor, at the dentist's office. Start a conversation.

c. Another day, you return to the dentist for another visit. Your neighbor's son (Ralph Smith) walks in. You have a toothache. Ralph is holding his chin with his right hand and some ice. You notice a little blood.
d. Your other neighbor's son, Jorge Martinez, has a sore throat.
e. Jorge Martinez broke his left leg (he was using a razor scooter and he fell.)
f. You are sitting outside your house and you see Ralph. He is bicycling and he falls. He scrapes his leg. You bring a paper towel and some water.
g. Ralph fell near your swimming pool. He knocked his head and now he's at the bottom of the pool. He's not moving. Do you know CPR? (car____ pulm_____ resus_____)
h. An electric line is down and it has been raining. Jorge runs over to your house and shouts, "My friend is getting an electric shock. Can you help pull him off?" (Do some investigation: Call the local fire department and ask for advice-what is the best way to pull someone away from a live electric line?)
i. Your neighbor runs up to your house and shouts, "A snake bit Jorge. The snake makes a sound like bzzzzzzz with its tail. Can you help?"
j. A dog bit Ralph, your neighbor's son, and he's crying. What should you say? Who will you call?

Situation # 2 (Health)
Ignacio needs to get health insurance for his two daughters. He asked the father of one of his daughter's classmates. Where should he go? What are the prices for an insurance policy and which things does it cover? Write a conversation between the two fathers.

2.15
FIND THE ERRORS
Here is a composition that Alejandro wrote. Can you find the errors?
Last night Mariale (my 13 daughter), broke a glass in the kitchen, my baby daughter was there too, without shoes and cut her small finger

(the smallest finger of this home...!!!), it blooded. I was sleeping, I had had a happy, long and exhaustive day.

I woke up, I saw my finger's baby blooding, my son was helping her, so I went back to sleep.

My family wasn't happy with my attitude (but I was very tired, I couldn't do anything else)

Hours later, I wake up worried, thinking that my son made a tight cure. I checked my baby, I saw the cure was very well fixed. I breath, I went to the pc....and...here we are.

The teacher will make some _____ (REPAIRS, CORREC-TIONS, IMPROVEMENTS)
Use these nouns as verbs:
I will _____ your composition
The teacher _____ the composition

ANSWERS: Repair, correct, improve. Fix is also a good verb.
Here are the corrections:
WAIT—-the baby's feet were not covered. So the "finger of the foot" is a ____.
Last night Mariale (my 13-year-old daughter) broke a glass in the kitchen. My baby daughter was there, too, without shoes and she cut her small finger (she has the smallest finger of this home...!!!). It bled. I was sleeping when this happened. I had had a happy, long and exhaustive day.

I woke up, I saw my baby's bleeding finger and I saw that my son was helping her, so I went back to sleep.

NOTE FROM THE TEACHER: I saw my baby's bleeding toe. The word "toe" should replace "finger."

My family wasn't happy with my attitude, but I was very tired. I couldn't do anything else).

Hours later, I woke up worried, thinking that my son made a tight bandage. I checked my baby, I saw the bandage was very well fixed. I breathed deeply, I was relieved, so I went to the PC….and…here we are.

HERE ARE SOME QUESTIONS:

I am a golfing guy……………………..is it well said?

When can I use the ing…for verbs…or…activities?

Ex. I like golfing, I like swimming, I like driving, I go shopping,

TEACHER'S ANSWER: YES-these are THINGS and activities.

VERBS: In this photo, you can see that I am golfing.

When you watch something on TV: "Look, he is cooking a dog!"

-ing is for an action that is continuing to happen.

Also for the past…I was sleeping when my daughter cut her finger.

When you want to say "I'm a golfing guy", you can say "I'm a golfer"

You can use-ing for an adjective

It is a hot day

It is a day for golf It is a golfing day

ANSWERS

These are the corrections for the READING at the beginning of the Chapter.

"The medical service is something that cannot be fair. It has to be excellent."

NOTE: In U.S. English, the period (.) goes inside the second quotation mark:…has to be excellent." NOT has to be excellent".

Also: The medical service cannot be average or mediocre. It has to be excellent.

In Venezuela, there are so many health problems, overcoat in the rural zones of the country, due to the bad quality that the public hospitals have. Really, the problem is economic. Those hospitals are subsidized by the government, or should be subsidized by it, but they don't pay the doctors, and the hospitals don't have any founds to buy the necessary materials and instruments, so the attention to the patients is very bad, and that causes many epidemical diseases in the rural population. I'm going to talk about one specific disease: ancylostomiasis. That's an intestinal disease caused by one parasite that rural people catch through faeces in the soil. That disease is very serious, because the parasite develops in the person, it grows, and causes many problems, like anemia, weakness, and also death in some cases. People cannot go to any hospitals to receive treatment, because they are badly attended because of the shortage of materials, or simply there are no doctors who work without charge.

The MSAS (Ministerio de Sanidad y Asistencia Social) has completed a lot of studies to know the number of people with each disease and those numbers have increased notably in the last 20 years, due to the public health problem in the country.

2.16

A Special Section on Food

Where can we talk about food? Food is part of Fun (Chapter 10) and part of our Family (Chapter 5). Well, let's follow the wisdom of the ancient people who said, "Let food be your medicine and let medicine be your food." Let's talk a little about food in this chapter.

There are some recipes on the web that some students created and some interesting stories about food. Go to www.teacherstoteachers.com and click on FEB 2001 for the recipes.

Here's an example of one of the "Origins of Words"

From: Maria Teresa Bannwart [mailto:bannwart@uol.com.br]

Maybe your students will find it interesting to know the origin of some words. So, here it goes: KETCHUP comes from the word ketsiap, a fish spicy vinegary sauce used in China during the 17th Century. English merchants took that exotic sauce home. Time changed the formula. By the end of 18th Century, at the northeast part of the USA, tomatoes were added to the recipe, resulting in the taste we know nowadays.

How can we remember the directions on a map? In French they are Nord, Sud, Est and Ouest. In Spanish the directions are Norte, Sur, Este y Oeste. Well, you get NEWS in English. It's made of the initials of North, East, West and South, meaning that the information is from all parts of the world. I hope it can be useful.
Love and kisses,
Mate
(Mate was a student at TALK International School of Languages in Fort Lauderdale in February 2001. She's from Brazil and she hopes people will write to her at bannwart@uol.com.br with interesting stories about the origins of words.)

2.17
Too much food?
There is an interesting diet program that one of my students uses and she is muy flaca now! (very thin, not fat)

You can see the diet at www.teacherstoteachers.com and then click on "8 weeks" and then you look for the link to GOOD DIET.

OPTIONAL PRACTICE
There is an exercise to practice shopping in the VOCABULARY section of Chapter 10 (Fun).

ANSWERS
COBRA Consolidated Omnibus Budget Reconciliation Act
OSHA Occupational Safety and Health Administration
HMO Health Maintenance Organization
RN Registered Nurse

You can find other abbreviations on the web site. Go to the ESL BOOK page, then click on Chapter 2. Look for "abbreviations."

3. Transportation

There are photos for this chapter at *www.teacherstoteachers.com*, then click on "ESL BOOK" and click on "Chapter 3."

3.1
PAIR WORK (CONVERSATION): Here are some words that you need to know. Work with your partner and write a sentence with each word or phrase (if you don't understand the words, your teacher can explain them):
Road Rage
Congestion
A hitchhiker
A flat tire
A dead battery
A spare tire
A fender bender
Tailgate
Alternative route

3.2
PAIRWORK: Work with your partner and answer these questions.
How can I get my license?
How do people get around in your country?
What is the price of gasoline in your country?
Do you have questions about the bus system in the USA?
What surprised you when you came to the USA about transportation?

Describe a problem that you had in the USA.

What did you do?

Do you have any recommendations?

3.3

READING and DISCUSSION

Talk with your partner about these responses by ESL students:

How do people get around in your country?

What is the price of the gasoline in your country?-Most of the people get around in their own cars, but there is a lot of people that get around in public transportation or on foot.

-People use Transmilenio System in Bogota (buses between cities). Cars, for the cities and roads…..train is not very common……and airplanes.

In Venezuela:

-The cheapest…………….Bs. 40…………$0.05

-The medium………………Bs. 55…………$ 0.08

-The most expensive……...Bs. 70…………$ 0.10

This is per liter.

In Colombia

-A little big more expensive than in USA……US $ 1.60

In Korea

-The price of gasoline in my country is US $ 2.50

In Dominican Republic

-In my country, the gasoline is about $ 2 per gallon.

How can I get my driver license?

-Go to the D.L.O (DMV = Department of Motor Vehicles), wait in line, get your number, and answer your exam on the computer. After that, take the practice exam. They'll take your photo in 20 minutes, and they give you your driver license.

Do you have questions about the bus system in the USA?
1 How frequently do the buses run?
2 Is there some bus system in the NSU?
3 How can I go to Nova University from Pembroke Pines?
4 I don't know the different routes and where can you find information about it?
5 What is the longest distance covered by a bus company in the USA?
6 For what reason do the people have to wait 20 or 30 minutes to take a bus?
Can you try to answer these questions? Answers are tat the end of the chapter.

What surprised you when you came to the USA about transportation?
-I didn't see any bus on the street, In my country (Venezuela), there are almost the same quantity of buses as cars. Here I haven't seen many public buses for transportation.
-The place where I live, doesn't have public transportation (buses, metro…..)
-Taxis are very expensive
-Small cities don't have public transportation
-The transportation in the USA is very effective, and it operates well.
-The roads and the highways are excellent, and they have good maintenance.
-They are very rigids about the laws for driving.
(it is "rigid"………..never "rigids").

Describe a problem that you had in the USA. What did you do?
-I had some problems speaking in English with some drivers. I tried to solve the situation by trying to remember the appropriate words to use.
-Once, I was driving in the highway, and a car came suddenly very close to mine so fast….I was scared, but fortunately the car went away, and I didn't have any accident.

Do you have any recommendations?

-Everybody has a car here. The distances between the places are too long, so if you are thinking about staying here more than 6 months, it's better to buy a car. It could be used (pre-owned, secondhand), and you can pay for it with cash, or it can be new, and you can make payments for a lot of time. But for the second option you need a social security number, so they can approve your credit.

-Take care when you drive, and be responsible with the others drivers.

-Take your time when you drive

-Look at the yellow pages for taxis.

-Take the exam for the driver license: read carefully and "learn" each chapter of the book.

3.4

ABBREVIATIONS

What is STP? What does the abbreviation stand for?

MPH

RPM

RR

ST

TER

PL

AVE

BLVD

WY

HWY

Ask your teacher for the answers. Or look on the web site www.teacherstoteachers.com, then click on ESL and go to the table of contents and look under Chapter 3. :)

3.5

ADVICE: "It's a good idea to..."

1. get a car in the USA. The bus system is not extensive or reliable.
2. avoid driving through certain areas. Ask your teacher to tell you areas that are dangerous at night or where drug-dealing occurs.
3. carry a tool in your car to break the window. If your car falls into a canal, how will you get out? (There is one answer at the end of this chapter.)
4. carry an extra key (a sp____re) in your wallet.
5. POLICE: If a police officer stops your car, please keep your hands (BOTH hands) on the steering wheel. If your windows have dark tinting, roll down the window and put both hands back on the wheel. If you think the officer is not a real officer, shout to him that you are moving slowly to a public place. Then move slowly with your lights blinking to show that you are not running away. (If you have questions about this, please talk with your teacher or write to a police officer. It's important that the police officer knows that you are not running away, so write this note: "I want to move to a public place." (If he doesn't agree, perhaps he is not a police officer.) (Yes, this information was at the beginning of this book, but it is very important, so please read it again! Do you have a pen and paper)
ANSWER to number 4 above: a spare key.

3.6
INTERNET: "Here are some internet sites for you to visit to find more information."
(If you know about other web sites, please send a message to english-lesson@mail.com and we will consider adding your suggestion to our web site.)
www.broward.org/bct/fixed.htm
Find a route on the Broward County bus system.

www.co.miami-dade.fl.us/mdta/
Find a route on the Miami bus system.

www.apta.com/sites/transus/bus.htm
Find a route on another city's bus system.

Visit this web site for more information that was submitted by students: www.geocities.com/talkinternational/transportation.html

Do you have your own web site? There is an easy program to learn called "geocities.com" and you can get a two-page list of instructions at *www.geocities.com/countries2001/instruction.html*. Good luck! Send us your page's link!

3.7
OPTIONAL ACTIVITY
Visit this website: *www.virtourist.com*. Click on an interesting country and look at the photos.
Write a composition and mail it to englishlesson@mail.com. We'll look at the composition and we'll make some corrections. If you want, we will send the composition to a local student newspaper for publication. For example, you can send the article to nsunews@nova.edu and the editor will evaluate the article.

3.8
LETTER: "Write a letter to the manager of the car repair shop to explain your problem. Ask for something. Ask for help." Then show the letter to your teacher.

3.9
LISTENING
On the CD-1, available from www.teacherstoteachers.com, you can listen to the conversation. With your partner, listen to ten sentences,

write down the entire sentences and then show the sentences to your teacher.

3.10
OPTIONAL Listening exercise:
Call 777-FILM (What are the numbers for this? F = __, I = __, L = __, M = __) and listen to the recording. Work with your partner. Take turns listening on the phone or ask to use a speakerphone. This is also a good listening exercise for homework. Look at the end of the chapter to find the answers to these questions

What is the first sentence?
"Welcome to _____ Movie phone."

What are the options?
Press 1 to _____ the movie you want to see
Press 2 to br____se
Press 3 for information about a th_____
Press 4 to hear the _____ of the week
Press 5 if you are using Moviephone for _____
Press 6 for information about the sponsors (Who are the sponsors?)
Press 7 for information about r_____gs
Press 8 if you want information about _____
Press 9 for T_____s
Press 0 if you want information about _____
Answers are on the web site for ESL and at the end of this chapter.

3.11
GRAMMAR
Show your answers to your partner and then show the answers to your teacher.
its it's

the dog likes _____ bone
_____ hot today.

Which or THAT
The room, _____ I cleaned, is dirty again.
(extra information that is not important, and it is not restricted.)

The room _____ I cleaned is dirty again.
(important, specific information that restricts WHICH room)

their there they're
Did they do _____ homework?
_____ on the beach.
_____ is someone in the kitchen.

3.12
VOCABULARY
WATER:
Here's some good information for you. Drink to your health!
(Underline the words that you don't understand and ask your teacher
to explain them).

75% of Americans are chronically dehydrated.

In 37% of Americans, the thirst mechanism is so weak that it is often
mistaken for hunger.

Even MILD dehydration will slow down one's metabolism as much as
3%.

One glass of water shut down midnight hunger pangs for almost 100%
of the dieters studied in a U of Washington study.

Lack of water is the #1 trigger of daytime fatigue.

Preliminary research indicates that 8-10 glasses of water a day could significantly ease back and joint pain for up to 80% of sufferers.

A mere 2% drop in body water can trigger fuzzy short-term memory, trouble with basic math, and difficulty focusing on the computer screen or on a printed page.

Drinking 5 glasses of water daily decreases the risk of colon cancer by 45%, plus it can slash the risk of breast cancer by 79%, and one is 50% less likely to develop bladder cancer.

3.13
READING
Go to the local Post Office and ask for a "Consumer Information Catalog." There are over 80 catalogs that are free-you only need to ask for them. You can request them online at www.pueblo.gsa.gov or you can call 1-888 8 PUEBLO (1-888-878-3256). Find five new words in a booklet and ask your teacher to explain the words to you.

3.14
JOKE
A young businessman had just started his own firm. He'd rented a beautiful office and had it furnished with antiques. Sitting there, he saw a man come into the outer office. Wishing to appear busy, the businessman picked up the phone and started to pretend he had a big deal working. He threw huge figures around and made giant commitments. Finally, he hung up and asked the visitor, "Can I help you?" The man said, "Sure. I've come to install the phone!"

3.15

WRITE A DIALOG

Part A: Choose one of these situations and imagine the words that are said. Work with your partner.

Part B: Create another situation. Describe the situation and (if you want to) send it by e-mail to englishlesson@mail.com.

Transportation

a. You are cooking meat on the barbecue. It is Saturday evening and your neighbors are visiting you (Martinez and Smith families). Suddenly you hear a big crash. It sounds like a car has hit another car. You run to the front of your house. A large SUV smashed into your car. The person inside looks confused. Talk to the driver, your insurance agent, the police, the other neighbors, the hospital and the ambulance driver.

b. You need a car for one day. Your car is in the garage. You can call Enterprise rent-a-car because they offer to drive the car to you. Ask for the rate (use a phone with a speaker so that your partner can listen.) Write the dialog with the people you speak.

c. Police.... You were driving 10 miles per hour faster than the speed limit. The cop asks you to "pull over." Write a dialog that includes words like: hands on the steering wheel, registration, proof of insurance, driver's license.

d. You went through a red light.

e. Jorge turned right on a red light and there was a sign that reads "No Right On Red." Mrs. Martinez calls you and asks for help.

f. Jorge lost his car keys. He needs help getting into the car. (Lock smith, call and ask the cost of getting a car open and the cost of making a new key. Where can you keep an extra key for your car?)

Situation # 3 (Transportation)

Maria's car is broken. She lives alone and she needs to go to classes at Nova, and then, go to work to Miami. She lives in Plantation and she doesn't know how to take a bus or taxi from there. She doesn't know anyone well and she doesn't have the confidence to ask him/her to drive her...so what can she do?

If your car falls into a canal, how will you get out?
ANSWER: Before you get into your car, buy a tool called a "center punch." Ask for one that is loaded with a spring (it is a spring-loaded center punch). Always put on your seat belt. If your car falls into the water, take a deep breath when you go under. Your air bag might open! Do not open the car door until the car is resting on the bottom and some water has entered the car (it's hard to open the door if water is on only one side of the car). Wait until there is water in the car. Slowly open the door. If you can't open the door, find the tool for breaking the window (a center punch). Break a side window (the front window is designed to hold together during a crash, so it will not easily fall apart). Swim to the surface.

If there is another person in the car, get another breath, check the location of the car, shout for help, take another deep breath and dive again. Do you have other suggestions? A firefighter and a paramedic checked this procedure, but you might have other information.

ANSWERS FOR 777-FILM
Welcome to AOL Movie phone.
Press 1 to select the name of the movie you want to see
Press 2 to browse
Press 3 for information about a theater
Press 4 to hear the movie pick of the week
Press 5 if you are using Moviephone for the first time
Press 6 for information about the sponsors (Y-100, American Express)
Press 7 for information about ratings
Press 8 **
Press 9 for show content and tickets
Press 0 **
**I'm sorry, you have made an invalid selection.

If this information is no longer useful, please write to englishlesson@mail.com and we'll put the correct information on the web site for ESL at www.teacherstoteachers.com then click on "ESL BOOK."

Do you have questions about the bus system in the USA?

1 How frequently do the buses run? Usually every 30 minutes in Broward County.

2 Is there some bus system in the NSU? In Nova Southeastern University there isn't a bus system, but between the campuses of Florida Atlantic University there is a bus system.

3 How can I go to Nova University from Pembroke Pines? By bus? Maybe you can call the bus system at 357-8400.

4 I don't know the different routes and where can you find information about it? You can visit the web site for the Broward County Transit. *www.broward.org/bct/fixed.htm*. Find a route on the Broward County bus system..

5 What is the longest distance covered by a bus company in the USA? Greyhound Bus goes across the USA.

6 For what reason do the people have to wait 20 or 30 minutes to take a bus? The bus system is not funded enough to have more frequent buses.

4. Multicultural Issues

There are photos for this chapter at *www.teacherstoteachers.com*, then click on "ESL BOOK" and click on "Chapter 4."

4.1
PAIR WORK-A CONVERSATION : Here are some words that you need to know. Work with your partner and write a sentence with each word or phrase:
The Typical U.S. attitude toward Money
Work
Vacations (2 weeks. In Europe, 4 to 6 weeks)
Time
Waiting in Line
Can you think outside the box?
Can you follow the rules?
Can you wait?
Can you please go away?
Can you ignore this problem?
Rule Number 1: The customer is always right.
Rule Number 2: when the customer is wrong or when the customer annoys (bothers, irritates) you, please remember Rule Number 1.

4.2
PAIRWORK: Work with your partner and answer these questions.
Do you have questions about the social systems in the USA?
What is polite in your country? What is different in the USA?
What surprised you when you came to the USA about people's behaviors?

Describe a problem that you had in the USA.
What did you do?
Do you have any recommendations?

READING and DISCUSSION
Talk with your partner about these responses by ESL students:
Do you have questions about the social system in the USA?
-Which ones are the holidays here?
-How many vocational periods do you have in a year?
-When you have to complain…………..what's the best way to do it?

What is polite in your country? What is different in the USA?
-The behavior of the people is very different. In my country the men are more gentleman than here. In general, the people here is more liberal. In my country is polite to open the door to the women, pay in a restaurant…etc.
-People's greeting and courtesy is very usual in the Dominican Republic.
-The relationships between people in Venezuela are better than in the USA. One reason is the racism. In the USA I have seen many cases of racism.
-In Colombia it's polite to say "thank you", to be flexible with people, to be patient. Even though, I think that people here are more polite and patient that in my country.
-In my country, it's polite to be a responsible person, with good feelings and sociable. The people here are in the same way than us, but they are colder.

What surprised you when you came to the USA about people's behaviors?
-Here, the people "in general" has another mind. The women can open the door, and pay for their food…..etc. That's terrible for someone in my country, but that's what the people say here…I have heard it.
-People respect the other people's lifestyle. I like that behavior.

-I surprised when I arrived to my house here for first time. I greeted my neighbor, and she asked me, and said "hello"......I can't believe it.
-Americans are focused people.
-They are more organized than Latin American people.
-They respect all the laws.
-Teenagers don't respect teachers, and sometimes they respond back to their parents.

Describe a problem that you had in the USA. What did you do?
-I have had only the problem to understand the people in the stores or by phone...US people talk too fast. I have tried to pay attention carefully to the people when they talk, and doing listening exercises with cassettes and TV.
-I feel so bad when I heard some kind of discrimination about the Latins, but I tried to not give it importance, because I'm very proud about my origin.

Do you have any recommendations?
-If you are going to stay here for study or for work, try to meet friends, because if you are here alone, it's very difficult to endure the situation.
-Teenagers have to respect older people.

4.3
ABBREVIATIONS
What is SWF? What does the abbreviation stand for?
DWM
MWC
BUPPY
YUPPIE
YUCA
To find the answers, go to www.teacherstoteachers.com, then click on ESL book and then click on the chapter that you want to look at (Chapter 4).

4.4

ADVICE: "It's a good idea to…"

It's a good idea to keep a map near you in a class. When you meet someone from another country, ask, "Where is your city? Please show it to me on your map. And where is a good place to visit in your country?"

When you show an interest in another country, the person is very optimistic and he has a positive feeling after talking with you.

4.5

INTERNET: "Here are some internet sites for you to visit to find more information."

(If you know about other web sites, please send a message to englishlesson@mail.com and we will consider adding your suggestion to our web site.)

The Broward School Board has 8 principles that are universal and they help bring cultures together. The web site is found by going to www.browardschools.com then click on CHARACTER. (The Core of our Lives)

www.browardschools.com/maincentr/character.html

Visit this web site for more information that was submitted by students: www.geocities.com/talkinternational/culture.html

4.6

LETTER: "Write a letter to the manager of the bank to explain a multicultural problem. For example, the manager is a white male who was born in New York City and he doesn't understand why the celebration on Calle Ocho is an important day for you. Ask for something. Explain why you want a day off to attend a festival that is important for your family." Then show the letter to your teacher.

4.7
LISTENING: On the CD-1, available from www.teacherstoteachers.com, you can listen to the conversation. With your partner, listen to ten sentences, write down the entire sentences and then show the sentences to your teacher.

4.8
GRAMMAR
Show your answers to your partner and then show the answers to your teacher.

beard bird beer
He is drinking a _____.
Do you hear the _____ singing?
He has a grey ____ .

to two too
I want to go, ____!
I will go ____ school
_____ children went to school.

lanes lines
The street has two solid or unbroken _____ and three broken _____ and so it has four _____.

4.9

VOCABULARY: Here are the eight words of the core curriculum of Broward County's public schools.

Can you change the word from a "THING" to an "ADJECTIVE"?

He has _____. He is a _____ man.

He has responsibility. He is a responsible man.

Continue with these words:

Kindness

Respect

Honesty

Self-control

Tolerance

Cooperation

Citizenship

4.10

READING: Subscribe to an internet e-letter and receive a new vocabulary lesson each week.

"Quotes of the Day" <qotd@starlingtech.com>

Motivational Quotes of the Day: We are all here for a spell; get all the good laughs you can.—Will Rogers

First learn the meaning of what you say, and then speak.—Epictetus

There is one piece of advice, in a life of study, which I think no one will object to; and that is, every now and then to be completely idle-to do nothing at all.—Sydney Smith

Press on: nothing in the world can take the place of perseverance. Talent will not; nothing is more common than unsuccessful men with talent. Genius will not; unrewarded genius is almost a proverb.

Education will not; the world is full of educated derelicts. Persistence and determination alone are omnipotent.—Calvin Coolidge. For more quotes, visit The Quotations Page www.quotationspage.com/ or visit this web site: www.topica.com/lists/mqotd.

4.11
OPTIONAL READING
Here is something that was found on the Internet:

Immigrant Children—Stages of Adaptation for Immigrant Children
Silent Stage: This occurs when the child first arrives in a new country fearful, lonely, may last up to 1-2 years.

Uprooting Stage: In this stage the child's survival instincts are awakened realizes that her/his culture clashes with the new culture. The child experiences mixed emotions: excitement/fear, curiosity, loneliness.

Culture Shock: Results from a loss of all familiar signs, symbols, and cues of their original culture characterized by depression and confusion.

Acculturation or Assimilation: The adaptation may take one of two courses at this point.

Acculturation: If the child acculturates, he/she becomes part of the mainstream culture while still holding onto customs and values of his/her original culture.

Assimilation: If the child assimilates, he/she gives up his/her cultural values and beliefs and adopts the new cultural values in their place. People in this stage tend to believe that they must give up their own culture in order to fit into the mainstream culture.

Mainstream Stage: Those who successfully acculturate accept and integrate parts of both cultures into their lives. Children who typically display success in school have usually successfully acculturated. Other children have two separate selves—split between home life (original culture) and his/her out-of-home life (new mainstream culture)—they have not integrated the two cultures. These children may experience fear of embarrassment or lack of acceptance for their original culture in the mainstream culture. (Information adapted from a lecture about immigrant children provided by Anne Geroski.)

4.12

WRITE A DIALOG

Part A: Choose one of these situations and imagine the words that are said. Work with your partner.

Part B: Create another situation. Describe the situation and (if you want to) send it by e-mail to englishlesson@mail.com.

Multicultural Issues

a. Mrs. Smith comes to your house and asks for some advice. "I have a new neighbor who says she's from Egypt. She is not eating anything this month during the day time. Something about Ram a Dan." Explain the situation to her.

b. Mrs. Smith is arguing with Mr. Smith. You are cutting your hedge so you can hear everything they say but you can't be seen. They are talking about the Martinez people. You hear some terrible things. Mr. Smith is very bigoted, angry, unhappy about immigrants. What do you hear? (use words like "goddamn immigrants" and "wet backs" and "stupid morons" and "those people come over here and make a lot of babies. It's ruining our cities." What are other negative things that you have heard U.S. people say about immigrants?)

c. Jorge Martinez, the teenager, hit a neighbor's cat with a rock. The cat was peeing on the ground in front of Jorge's house. Mrs. Martinez asks for your help in translating...The neighbor called the police. The

Policeman says that there is no crime in hitting a cat with a rock. (use sentences like "next time, use a hose.")

Situation # 4 (Multicultural Issues)
Cristina went to a party last night and she was embarrassed for not knowing if it was "in good taste" to kiss the people on the cheek to greet them but they didn't answer her very well. What can you recommend to her, or advise her about the people's customs here?

5. Family

There are photos for this chapter at *www.teacherstoteachers.com*, then click on "ESL BOOK" and click on "Chapter 5."

5.1
READING (PAIRWORK)
This is a composition that a student wrote. With your partner or by yourself, find the errors. Then write your response to the questions.

Family
Each country has its own family system, and its customs. In Venezuela it is an old custom to live in your house with your parents until you get married, that is for the women, and for the men too. For that reason, the families are very united. Also it is common to meet in a house to celebrate the holidays like Christmas, New Year, birthdays, etc. It is not common, for example, to go to a New Year's party on December 31st. All the families are together in their houses and they do a private celebration.

Another thing that is customary in my country is to share the eating time with all the family. The lunch time is the most important meal. During lunch, you tell the others about your things, what you did, who you are with, etc.

I think here, in the USA there's not time to do that at lunch, but I think the families could do it at night. A good relationship with the family is very important and it's even more important if the guys and girls leave their houses at a young age to live alone. (The corrections are at the end of this chapter.)

5.2
QUESTIONS
What is the custom in your country on December 31?
When does your family eat together?

PHOTO 5.1 These students are on vacation with Carlos Schulz. What are these students going to write to their parents? Imagine that you are one of these students and write a letter. You can see this photo on www.virtourst.com/keywest.

5.3
PAIR WORK (CONVERSATION): Here are some words that you need to know. But these words are in Spanish! Translate these words into English, then work with your partner and write a sentence with each word or phrase:
Nietos
Sobrinas
Primas
Abuelo
Tio
Adjectives: helpful, encouraging, generous, always there, late, early,…
Verbs: cook, clean, pay the bills, catch, throw, carry, hide, play, work,…

Work with your partner and find five more words about "family." Show your list to your teacher and to another pair of students. Write five sentences using some of these words.

5.4
PAIRWORK: Work with your partner and answer these questions.
How do people spend time with family in your country?
Do you have questions about the family system in the USA?
What surprised you when you came to the USA about families?
Describe a problem that you had in the USA.
What did you do?
Do you have any recommendations?

ANSWERS:
Nietos grandsons and granddaughters
Sobrinas nieces
Primas cousins
Abuelo grandfather
Tio uncle

Draw your family tree and show it to your partner. Tell a story about each person on your family tree.

5.5
READING and DISCUSSION
Talk with your partner about these responses by ESL students:
How do people spend time with family in your country?
The people in my country are very familiar and friendly. It is usual when neighbors talk to each other. Families are very close. They go to the parents' house and have dinner or lunch with them, usually once a week. The parents are really important there. People go to their farms if there is a long weekend. Some people go out to eat. Generally the families eat together at lunch and at dinner. In my family we go to the beach together, to a restaurant or to a movie. We enjoy watching a movie together or simply talking about anything.

What surprised you when you came to the USA about families?

CONVERSATION

DISCUSS THESE ANSWERS WITH YOUR PARTNER. DO YOU AGREE? WHY?

When the young people turn 16 or 17 they leave the house and look for a future by themselves.

The families are too selfish.

They are very independent and liberal.

I think in USA the people don't have time to share, because the household chores are so hard. In my country, we are helped by many employees daily.

Both parents are working and the children are alone for a lot of time.

Each member of a family here is independent. Each one does his or her own things. They have lunch out of the house and sometimes they have dinner separately. The children move to live in another place at a young age (at 18 years old).

Do you have questions about the family system in the USA?

CONVERSATION: DISCUSS THESE QUESTIONS WITH YOUR PARTNER. WRITE ANSWERS IF YOU KNOW THE ANSWERS

Is the new US family system (two parents who work, the children never eat with the parents) really positive for the children's future?

Until what age do the children live with their parents (usually)?

How do the families share the house?

What is the most common age to get married?

For some answers, go to the website www.geocities.com/talkinternational/family.html

Describe a problem that you had in the USA. What did you do?

CONVERSATION: DO YOU AGREE WITH THE SOLUTION?

When I wanted to rent an apartment, they limited the number of children…it was one of the conditions for renting the apartment. SOLUTION: I looked for another apartment without limits of the number of children for living in the apartment.

When I first came to the USA to stay with my uncle, I was lost about their customs. It took me time to adapt to them. We only have dinner together, so we don't see each other very much during the day.

MORE CONVERSATION: CAN YOU SUGGEST A SOLUTION? Work with your partner.
Do you have any recommendations?
Know the families' behavior and try to understand their lifestyle.

It's a good idea for the family to try to spend time together. You can get to know each other and share the evenings together. At least spend Sunday together.

Please send your suggestions to englishlesson@mail.com and we will put the best ones on our web site for FAMILY.

5.6
ABBREVIATIONS: Work with your partner to answer these questions
Do you know these abbreviations?
DINK
GRUMPY
YUPPIE
BUPPIE
Write more abbreviations that you don't understand. Ask the teacher for the answers. (Or look at the end of this chapter.)

5.7
ADVICE: "It's a good idea to…"

1. It's a good idea to remind your family to drink more water.

2. It's a good idea to go for a walk together in the evening, when the family has calmed down. Turn off the TV and spend 15 minutes walking under the stars together.

3. It's a good idea to smile…take turns going to a web side that creates funny jokes that all of the family can enjoy. *www.lablaughs.com.* You can also go to www.jokes.com and click on "children".

4. It's a good idea to look closely at a web page before you conclude that it is true. Look at these web pages and tell me if they are true:

A. Bonsai Kittens

"Look what it is been done to the kittens in New York….it's terrible!!!!! And somebody made a web page about it. Read the method that they use, and don't look at the gallery if you don't want to cry. This is very sad, and I'm sending it to you in order to spread the news. The web page is www.bonsaikitten.com."

B. People who look for water with sticks = "dowsers"

Some dowsers will insist that rubber footwear must be used by the operator, while an equal number insist that such materials inhibit the effect, and must never be used. Every dowser has his or her own personal theory, rules and preferred techniques.

Some claim that their power is divine in nature. Some say that dowsing is a learned art. Most claim that anyone can dowse successfully, while others say that it is an inherited gift. Some deny that it is in any way "paranormal," while some embrace that definition. Some say that they can only perform successfully if there is a real "human need" present; others are not so inhibited. Many say that they can find any object or substance, while others say they can find, for example, only flowing water moving underground, but not in pipes. Most dowsers claim 100% accuracy. Very few claim anything less than 90%. www.randi.org/research/challenge/dowsing.html

C. Photographs of fairies.

In 1917 two innocent-seeming English schoolgirls, 16-year-old Elsie Wright and her 10-year-old cousin Frances Griffiths, launched a deception that somehow managed to fool many people over the following years, including the creator of Sherlock Holmes, Sir Arthur Conan Doyle. While playing in Cottingley Glen, just behind the Wright home, the girls took what they claimed were close-up photographs of winged fairies dancing amid the foliage. The girls then took each other's picture with the wee creatures, and photo experts who were consulted said that the images were not double exposures nor had the negatives been altered.
www.randi.org/research/r-files/cottingley/index.html

Which of these web pages is true? Write to danibabe81@hotmail.com and she will tell you which ones are true and which ones are jokes. In general, there are more items like this at: www.randi.org/index.shtml

5.8
PAIRWORK: Can you give some more advice to people who move to the USA?

5.9
INTERNET: "Here are some internet sites for you to visit to find more information." (If you know about other web sites, please send a message to englishlesson@mail.com and we will consider adding your suggestion to our web site.)

www.family.com Skills: The Parent Problem Solver
Do you have questions about your child's behavior and development? Are you looking for the best parenting techniques? Whether you're struggling with a tempestuous toddler or a pimple-prone preteen, you can find the answers you need. Go to www.family.com

Visit this web site for more information that was submitted by students: www.geocities.com/talkinternational/family.html

Where do you want to go with your family? Well, many people want to go to Disney and Universal and Sea World! www.orlando.com

www.nasa.gov gives the schedule for the next Shuttle Launch (look for "LAUNCH" on the left side of the page).

The Broward County Humane Society, *www.browardhumane.com/ouran-frien.html*. Yes, you can "hug" a dog or cat online! Just visit this website. Then go to Griffin Road just west of I-95 and visit the animals in person! 2070 Griffin Road, Fort Lauderdale, FL 954 989 3977

www.pets4u.com a place for people to find animals!

Where can you find photos of cats and dogs?
www.i-love-cats.com and www.i-love-dogs.com
Food and family-a good combination. Write your mother's favorite recipes and send them to englishlesson@mail.com—I'll put them on the web site. (Or you can create a web site with your favorite recipes that your family uses and then send me the link to your web site.)

5.10
DO YOU KNOW THESE WORDS?
God bless America, Land that I love.
Stand b_____ her, and guide her,
Thru the n_____ with a light from a_____.
From the mountains, to the pr_____,
To the oceans, white with f_____-
God bless America! My home _____ home.
God bless America! My home _____ home.

You can find the answers at this web site: www.scoutsongs.com/lyrics/godblessamerica.html

5.11
DISCUSS WITH YOUR PARTNER
Let's pretend that you have a 16-year-old daughter. She went to walk the dog and she left her computer on. You walk in her room and you can see what she was looking at. The screen shows that the information is for dating and relationships: "Ask questions, read articles or take quizzes on dating and relationships." The name of this web site is dir.hotbot.lycos.com /Society /Relationships /Dating/
1. Do you want her to be visiting this web site?
2. What do you do?
3. If the child is a 16-year-old son, is your answer different?
4. At what age do the rules change? How old should a child be before he can look at this web site?

5.12
LETTER
CONVERSATION: Work with your partner: Talk to your partner about a problem with your family or a problem that you heard about in the newspaper. Write a letter to a friend to explain a problem you are having with someone in your family. Ask for help. Then show the letter to another pair of students.
OR
Imagine that Jorge Martinez is writing a letter to his parents to apologize for something that he did. Jorge is very, very, very sorry. (What did Jorge do? Use your imagination.) Then show the letter to your teacher.

5.13
LISTENING
On the CD-1, available from www.teacherstoteachers.com, you can listen to the conversation. With your partner, listen to ten sentences, write down the entire sentences and then show the sentences to your teacher.

Listen with your partner to a tape recording. Write a letter to the person who was speaking on the tape.

5.14
GRAMMAR: Fill in the blank. WORK WITH YOUR PARTNER.
He is a _____ man.
He is a _____.
He wants to _____
(succeed, success, successful).

Now write three sentences using these sets of words:
(angry, anger, anger)
(red, redden, red face)
(difficult, difficulty, verb + difficult)
(occupied, occupy, preoccupied)
(complicated, complicate, complication)
For answers, see the ESL BOOK web site (Chapter 5).

rip tear tear
There is a _____ on his cheek.
Look, there is a _____ in her dress.

bare bear
I want a teddy _____
I don't have shoes….I have _____ feet.

5.15
VOCABULARY: CONVERSATION Work with your partner to find words about the family. Think of 10 words to describe a father and a mother. Give two synonyms for "kind." (a kind father). Write the opposite.
Here is a start: happy, considerate, helpful, caring, busy, tired, overwhelmed,…
Now take your list to the white board and put five of the words on the board.
EACH PAIR in the Class puts up 5 words.
ASK YOUR PARTNER and YOUR TEACHER: Do you understand all of the words on the board?
CONVERSATION AND PAIRWORK: Now write sentences using the words.

5.16
READING: Subscribe to an internet e-letter and receive a new vocabulary
lesson each week.

You can write for a free "joke each day"
To submit a joke, write to: Jokes@Laughshop.com.
To subscribe from this group, send an e-mail to: G-Jokes-subscribe@egroups.com

5.17
JOKE
The joke for this chapter comes from the humor of marriage.

I married Miss Right. I didn't know her first name was Always.

I haven't spoken to my wife for 18 months. I don't like to interrupt her.

Marriage is a 3-ring circus: Engagement ring, wedding ring, and suffering.

Why do men die before their wives? They want to.

Do you know the punishment for bigamy? Two mothers-in-law.

Young Son: Is it true, Dad, I heard that in some parts of Africa a man doesn't know his wife until he marries her?
Dad: That happens in every country, son.

A man inserted an 'ad' in the classified: "Wife Wanted". Next day he received a hundred letters.
They all said the same thing: "You can have mine."

The most effective way to remember your wife's birthday is to forget it once.

First guy (proudly): "My wife's an angel!"
Second guy: "You're lucky, mine's still alive."

How do most men define marriage? An expensive way to get laundry done for free.

Then there was a man who said, "I never knew what real happiness was until I got married; and then it was too late."

A little boy asked his father, "Daddy, how much does it cost to get married?"
And the father replied, "I don't know son, I'm still paying."

There are lots of differences between men and women. Look at what some people have written about gender differences (www.geocities.com/talkinternational/menandwomen.html). Please also look at chapter 13 in this book.

5.18
WORKSHEETS: Idioms, Proverbs, Phrasal verbs
The teacher can give you a worksheet.
OR
You and your partner can visit the list of idioms at www.geocities.com/talkinternational/roxana.html and write new sentences using five of the idioms.

Instructions for Life in the new millennium from the Dalai Lama:
1. Take into account that great love and great achievements involve great risk.
2. When you lose, don't lose the lesson.
3. Follow the three Rs: Respect for self, respect for others, responsibility for all your actions.
4. Remember that not getting what you want is sometimes a wonderful stroke of luck.
5. Learn the rules so you know how to break them properly.
6. Don't let a little dispute injure a great friendship.
7. When you realize you've made a mistake, take immediate steps to correct it.
8. Spend some time alone every day.
9. Open your arms to change, but don't let go of your values.
10. Remember that silence is sometimes the best answer.
11. Live a good, honorable life. Then when you get older and think back, you'll be able to enjoy it a second time.
12. A loving atmosphere in your home is the foundation for your life.
13. In disagreements with loved ones, deal only with the current situation. Don't bring up the past.

14. Share your knowledge. It's a way to achieve immortality.

15. Be gentle with the earth.

16. Once a year, go someplace you've never been before.

17. Remember that the best relationship is one in which your love for each other exceeds your need for each other.

18. Judge your success by what you had to give up in order to get it.

19. Approach love and cooking with reckless abandon.

(Permission was received to reprint this wisdom.)

PAIRWORK: With your partner, re-write four or five of these pieces of advice (above) and show the "rewording" to your teacher.

5.19

WRITE A DIALOG

Part A: Choose one of these situations and imagine the words that are said. Work with your partner.

Part B: Create another situation. Describe the situation and (if you want to) send it by e-mail to englishlesson@mail.com.

Family

a. You have a daughter. She wants to go out on a date with Ralph. You are worried about the condition of Ralph's car and you are not sure that he is an experienced driver. Talk to Mr. Smith, Ralph's father.

b. You are having a huge party next weekend and you don't have enough space for ice and the extra cakes. You ask your neighbor if you can use his refrigerator. (Your neighbor will be out of town, but you have a key to their house.)

c. Mrs. Martinez' mother died yesterday. She wants to put an ad in the newspaper. (Call the newspaper to find out the cost of an ad and how much time is needed to put the obituary in the newspaper.)

Situation # 5 (Family)

Anna is Carlos' daughter. She is 18 years old and she wants to live alone….she says that she can survive by herself if she can work, and that she needs more freedom. Carlos (her father) is terrified and he doesn't know what to do, because she tells him that everybody here does it....and there isn't anything wrong.

ANSWERS to the Reading at the beginning of the chapter.
The reading is in standard U.S. English. There is no correction.

5.20
PAIRWORK
Here is another reading about "family"-write a short note to Daniela danibabe81@hotmail.com and tell her your reactions to these pieces of advice.
-Don't cry over anyone who won't cry over you.
-Good friends are hard to find, harder to leave, and impossible to forget.
-You can only go as far as you push!
-Actions speak louder than words.
-The hardest thing to do is to watch the one you love when he or she loves somebody else.
-Don't let the past hold you back, you're missing the good stuff.-Life's short. If you don't look around once in a while you might miss it.
-A best friend is like a four-leaf clover, hard to find and lucky to have.
-Some people make the world special by just being in it.
-Best friends are the siblings God forgot to give us.
-When it hurts to look back, and you're scared to look ahead, you can look beside you and your best friend will be there.
-True friendship never ends.
-Friends are forever.
-Good friends are like stars....you don't always see them, but you know they are always there.
-What do you do when the only person who can make you stop crying is the person who made you cry?
-Nobody is perfect until you fall in love with them.

-Everything is okay in the end. If it's not okay, then it's not the end.
7 Most people walk in and out of your life, but only friends leave foot-
prints in your heart.
(This list was found by Daniela P.)

ANSWERS
DINK double income, no kids
GRUMPY grandparents who are upwardly mobile and professional
YUPPIE Young urban professional
BUPPIE black urban professional

6. House

There are photos for this chapter at *www.teacherstoteachers.com*, then click on "ESL BOOK" and click on "Chapter 6."

6.1
READING
A Local's Guide to Paris

Many people hear the word "Paris" and they imagine a beautiful city. I live there. Let me tell you something unusual about my city that you might not know.

When you live in Paris, you should try to go out at a different time than most people. The morning traffic jam is horrible. The buses, the cars, the people on the subway-it's very crowded! The underground is full and people aren't kind. They are very stressed and aggressive. People run to take a train and they often bump into each other.

If you come in Paris, you must begin the morning at about 10 o'clock and the evening after eight. This way, you will avoid many of the crowds. You will have many activities if you go to the Bastille, you can eat in different restaurants such as Chinese, Japanese, American, Brazilian, etc. You can go to see expositions and sometimes museums are open until 10 p.m.

In the summer people play music in the street. We have the "Festival of music" on 22 June, the longest day of the year (Midsummer).

If you like to roller blade or roller skate, you can "roll" in a car-free zone near the Seine between 10 a.m. and 5 p.m. on Sundays. On Friday night you can roll around Paris with three or four thousand other rollerbladers. They start in Place d'Italie and they go through streets of Paris for two or three hours. It's very organized. The police help you if you have difficulties or if you get lost. The route changes each week On Sunday there is another roller blade gathering that starts at the Bastille and it goes to another part of Paris.

There are a lot of parades in July when there is a Carnival in the Forest of Vincennes. If you want in the summer you can see movies outside after 10 p.m. in the Parc of La Villette (little city).

I hope you will visit my city and try something new!

(This was written by one of Steve's students, but he misplaced her name and her e-mail address…but you can still write to englishlesson@mail.com with your comments and questions and we'll ask another student from Paris to reply to you…)

6.2
PAIR WORK (CONVERSATION): Here are some words that you need to know. Work with your partner and write a sentence with each word or phrase:
Repairs
Mortgage (see finance)
Handy man
The Lawn guy
Fix a crack in the tile
Put caulk along the edge of some tiles in the bathroom

6.3

PAIRWORK: Work with your partner and answer these questions.

How big is a typical house in your country?

Do you have questions about the housing system in the USA?

What surprised you when you came to the USA about houses?

Where is a safe place to live? Where is a place that you recommend that people should not go? (Example: It is a good idea not to go in the area between I-95 and 441 and between Broward and Sunrise Blvd.)

Describe a problem that you had in the USA.

What did you do?

Do you have any recommendations?

6.4

READING and DISCUSSION

Talk with your partner about these responses by ESL students:

How big is a typical house in your country?

-A regular house in Venezuela, could have 200-250 m2, with three bed rooms, a medium kitchen, two bathrooms, a medium dinner room and a family room.

-A typical house in Korea has 4 bedrooms and 5 bathrooms. It could have two or three stories.

-In Colombia, a typical house is around 2000 Ft. We have different conceptions in the Family room, because our houses are more formal, and sometimes the social areas are not used frequently.

-A typical house in Dominican Republic, in the big cities, has 3 or 4 bedrooms, 2 bathrooms and a huge patio and a spacious garden.

Do you have questions about the housing system in the USA?

-What is the most common here…..to rent or to buy a house or an apartment?

-Which one is the best area to live?

-If you buy a house…..how much mortgage do you have to pay?

-Is the potable water (in the tubes) chemically treated? (by our architect....of course!!!!)
-Are the artificial lakes salt or not?

What surprised you when you came to the USA about houses?
-They are separated of the industries, and gathered in communities, in some places. Also, the houses are very big, and the material of the walls and of the doors, is very soft. In Venezuela, all the walls are solid.....so, the construction is harder.
-I surprised when I saw that all the houses had air conditioner. Should be because of the hot or humid weather.
-The houses are mostly one story, but they are big.
-The walls aren't built for bricks. The construction system is really different.

Where is a safe place to live? Where is a place that you recommend that people should not go?
-I think the safest place to live is where I live, in Weston. I don't know many others places, only the near ones, but Weston is very quiet, the people is very nice; and there is a police checkpoint in each community.
-It's not recommendable to go in the area between I-95 and Route 7 in Miami, and generally west of I-95 to 31st Avenue in Broward County is not a pleasant area (except in Hollywood). Another rule or guideline is to be careful when you are between the railroad tracks, which run north-south.

Describe a problem that you had in the USA. What did you do?
-One day, I was cooking, and the kitchen was giving off a little big of smoke. Well, the fire alarm began to sound. I didn't know what to do, but fortunately the firemen came to my house by themselves.. I received them, and they fixed the alarm, because it was very sensitive.
-I pre-rented a condo here from my country. When I came here, to the condo's office, I was informed that it wouldn't be possible that I

moved until one month later. I tried to pursue them. I let them know about my baby, my whole family, etc....but it didn't matter.

Do you have any recommendations?
-Buy a house in a safe place, and near to a drug store, to a supermarket, and if it's possible.....to a mall. Here, the distances are too long, so it's better to have those places near to the house.
-It's better to have a house not very big, because here you don't have any help to clean and do the house work.
-If you are looking for a place to move, go to the supermarket and find a little book called "FOR RENT", there you can find too many places to choose according with the budget and necessities.
-About the rentals and the mortgages....don't trust. "You can get irresponsible people in everywhere" I thought that was unusual in USA, but it happen too.

Describe a problem that you had in the USA.
I had a problem with a toilet in my house. It was blocked and I tried pouring hot water down the drain. It did not fix the problem.

What did you do?
I called a plumber.

Do you have any recommendations?

OTHER RECOMMENDATIONS
I can recommend a good plumber: 4-Star at 954.767-8999. (Steve) For other recommendations, go to www.teacherstoteachers.com, click on ESL and then look for "Recommendations" under Chapter 6. Can you recommend a person who can help fix things that are broken around the house?

6.5
ABBREVIATIONS: What is D-I-Y? What does the abbreviation stand for?
ASAP
PIP insurance
Inc.
LLC
PA
Corp.
GmbH
S.A.

What are these area codes used for in telephone?
1-877
1-900
1-888
1-800
1-878

6.6
ADVICE: "It's a good idea to…" = IAGI
IAGI to carry your medicine with you.
It's a good idea to check the web site of a store. You can prepare for your visit to the store. Here is an example that we found on the internet: www.dhc.com, which is also www.target.com for the Target store.

Can I order merchandise online that I saw at my Target store?
Yes, you can use advanced search to search for the product or you can shop the online assortment by going to the target.com Shop page. target.com is adding products for purchase online weekly, so check back soon. To find the Target closest to you, see our Target store locator or call 1-800-800-8800.
What is your return policy?

If you are not fully satisfied with your Target purchase, return it to any Target store with the original sales receipt within 90 days. Target will exchange it, repair it, or offer you a refund based on your method of payment. Purchases made by check may be refunded as a merchandise voucher. Some items cannot be returned if opened. These items include Music, Movies, Computer Software, Video Games, Sports and Toy Collectibles. It may be necessary to ask for identification during any transaction. Merchandise purchased online at target.com may also be returned to a Target store or by mail with the original packing receipt within 90 days from the order date. Shipping charges will not be refunded.

To return a target.com purchase to a Target store, bring:

1. The item you wish to return and all packaging/accessories.
2. The entire original packing receipt.
3. A form of personal identification.

To find the Target store closest to you, see our Target store locator or call 1-800-800-8800.

To return a target.com purchase by mail:

1. Box up the item and include all packaging/accessories.
2. Enclose the original packing receipt and be sure to complete all necessary information.
3. Ship your package to:

target.com Return
200 Rivertown Drive
Woodbury, MN 55118

If you are returning an item for an exchange, you will receive your replacement item within 10 business days after we receive your return, provided the item is in stock. If you are requesting a refund, your credit card account will be credited within 2 business days after we receive your return.

6.7

INTERNET: "Here are some internet sites for you to visit to find more information."

(If you know about other web sites, please send a message to english-lesson@mail.com and we will consider adding your suggestion to our web site.)

www.geocities.com/novanewspaper/hotelpalace.html
Visit this web site. Where is it? What is the special activity at this hotel? Why is it a good place to stay?

Visit this web site for more information that was submitted by students: www.geocities.com/talkinternational/house.html

A good grammar web site at Purdue University
owl.english.purdue.edu

www.everythingaboutfood.com

6.8

LETTER: "Write a letter to the manager of the pesticide company to explain your problem (your house has termites). Ask for something. Ask for help."

Then show the letter to your teacher.

6.9

LISTENING: On the CD-1, available from www.teacherstoteachers.com, you can listen to the conversation. With your partner, listen to ten sentences, write down the entire sentences and then show the sentences to your teacher.

6.10

GRAMMAR: fill in the blank (Look for missing words and incorrect grammar):

which with witch whit

The _____ came in my dream last night. She had a long stick and she wore a black dress and pointed hat.

I am _____ two people.

the room, _____ I cleaned yesterday, is ready for you.

Check the answer with your teacher.

Use I or me or my or mine.

Susan and _____ went to the beach. We jumped in the water.

A fish saw _____ and it bit _____ foot.

Susan has her book and I have _____.

A large bird dropped something on Susan and _____. We were hit by something from a bird. Yes, it was wet. It was terrible.

6.11

VOCABULARY: Give two synonyms for "garbage." Write the opposite. (What IS the opposite? "valuable stuff"? trash, waste…things I want to keep)

Patient: It's been one month since my last visit and I still feel miserable.

Doctor: Did you follow the instructions on the medicine I gave you?

Patient: I sure did. The bottle said, "keep tightly closed."

Work with your partner to think of synonyms for "go up" and "go down". Show your sentences to your teacher.

1. Going up

Yesterday the cost of a book went up

…rose

…was raised by the publisher

…jumped
…bounced
…rebounded
…returned to the previous level
the price of the stock g_____ned 5 dollars

2. Going down
Yesterday the price of water dropped
…declined
…decreased
…fell
…went down
the price of the stock l___t five dollars.

3. Staying flat
there was no change
Yesterday the price of gasoline remained steady.

ANSWERS: gained and lost.
In class we read the business report from a newspaper. We saw many words and we learned some new ones. We decided that it is a good idea to read the business section each week, even if we read it only one time and we look for up words, down words, and flat words (no change).

6.12
WRITE A DIALOG
Part A: Choose one of these situations and imagine the words that are said. Work with your partner.
Part B: Create another situation. Describe the situation and (if you want to) send it by e-mail to englishlesson@mail.com.

House
a. There is a fire in the Smith's house. The Smiths are not at home but you have their phone number at work. The fire is coming from the garage and you notice the smoke because you are home with a bad cold. It is 11 a.m.
b. Jorge's baseball broke your window and then knocked over your television (and it also broke). You need to talk to the insurance agent and you need to buy a new TV, plus you need to get a new window. You can get actual estimates over the telephone (use the yellow pages and ask for an approximate estimate from the glass repair store).
c. You are at Home Depot. Start a conversation with the cashier. Talk about the weather, it is very busy today, That's a nice hairdo, you want to know if there are more small palm trees (you took the last one on the floor).
d. Shopping in general and neighbors: You meet a neighbor (Mr. Jones or Mr. Or Mrs. Smith or Mr. Martinez) at one of these stores. You start a conversation (It's _____ to see you. What _____ you doing here today? Or "That's a nice plant.") You meet the neighbor at the following places: at Home Depot, a grocery store, Broward Mall, galleria Mall, Sawgrass Mall, at the airport, at a bus stop, at the hospital, at the movies, at the bank, at a pharmacy, at the driver license office, at a restaurant, etc.
e. Start a conversation with a neighbor at the library.
f. Return a damaged item. For example, your new neighbor Mischka from Russia asks you for help. "I just bought this game yesterday. I brought it home and it has a broken leg and 5 pieces are missing. Can you help me to return it?"

Situation # 6 (House)
Everybody says that this is the hurricane season and Mrs. Smith is worried about it......she lives in Miami and her neighbor told her that she has to put some wood sticks over the windows to cover them. She doesn't know where to buy them, or how to put them up, and her kind neighbor explains to her. Start a conversation......

7. Immigration

There are photos for this chapter at *www.teacherstoteachers.com*, then click on "ESL BOOK" and click on "Chapter 7."

7.1
READING
The immigration of the USA is very strict, more than the immigration of others countries. It shouldn't scare you, the only thing that you have to do is to respect it, and to do everything legal.

There are several statuses here, that immigration allows to each person, depending on his/her position. You can be here with a tourist visa for 6 months or until the date that immigration has given you in the passport. With this kind of visa you can't get a job. The other kind of visa is the student one. With this one you can study in any institution until the date that immigration has signed it; the regular time is one year, and after that, you can extend the time, transferring it to another institution or proving that you need to continue studying. An example of this point is, for example, if you're studying for a mater's degree of some profession, and it takes you 2 years, you should ask for a letter to the university where it says that your master's degree program is two years instead of one.

The H-1 visa allows you to work, it's the work visa, and it gives you a social security number.
(by danibabe81@hotmail.com)

7.2
PAIR WORK (CONVERSATION): Here are some words that you need to know. Work with your partner and write a sentence with each word or phrase:
Visiting the USA for the first time.
The tourist visa
The work permit or the work visa
The other Visas (h-1, e-2, ???)
Residence (Green Card)
Social Security Number

7.3
PAIRWORK: Work with your partner and answer these questions.
What surprised you when you came to the USA about immigration?
Describe a problem that you had in the USA.
What did you do?
Do you have any recommendations?

7.4
READING and DISCUSSION
Talk with your partner about these responses by ESL students:
What surprised you when you came to the USA about immigration?
-They have many visas. Almost one, for each necessity.
-They are well organized, but you have to wait for a long line.

Describe a problem that you had in the USA. What did you do?
-I had a problem with my social security, because somebody stole my wallet with some of my papers, in Venezuela, and I want to get it again, but I don't remember its number. So I want to know if I can get it again just with my last name and maybe my address or something like that. I will appreciate it if you can help me. Carola M.

Do you have any recommendations?

-You have to have all your papers updated....like your passport, visa, etc. It's a good idea to keep a copy of your passport, visa and credit cards in a friend's house.

-You must have knowledge about all the laws of immigration.

7.5

ABBREVIATIONS

What is I-20? What does the abbreviation stand for?

FBI

CIA

INS

7.6

ADVICE: "It's a good idea to..." (IAGI)

IAGI to plan ahead.

IAGI to have a good lawyer.

IAGI to give the school plenty of time to renew the I-20 (at least 45 days)

IAGI to keep all of the telephone numbers that you need in a safe place.

IAGI to make a copy of your passport and the visa page!

7.7

INTERNET: "Here are some internet sites for you to visit to find more information."

(If you know about other web sites, please send a message to english-lesson@mail.com and we will consider adding your suggestion to our web site.)

The US Department of Justice maintains a good page: www.ins.usdog.gov/graphics/howdoi/academia.htm

www.ins.usdoj.gov/graphics/
That's another way to get into the web site.

www.jcampion-law.com
Jeff Campion has a useful web site. His "frequently asked questions" are helpful. His e-mail address is campionj@hotmail.com and his phone number is 954.764.6779, fax 764.6789.

7.8
LETTER
Write a letter to Jeff Campion to request a seminar about immigration. He might send a video tape of his standard talk. Then show the letter to your teacher.

7.9
LISTENING
"Listen to a video tape about immigration given by J. Campion."
(It is available from www.teacherstoteachers.com or you can contact Jeff Campion at campionj@hotmail..com) and invite him to speak to your class.

7.10
GRAMMAR
Use he or him or his:
Jim drove a car and picked up Susan. They looked at the blue sky and said, "Let's go outside." They decided to cancel their plan to go shopping.

Jim was excited.

Susan and ____ went to the beach. They jumped in the water.

Jim was not lucky when he went into the water.
A fish saw _____ and it bit _____ foot.

Susan has her book and Jim has _____.

Jim was not lucky when he returned to his car. A large bird dropped something on Susan and _____. They were hit by something from a bird. Yes, it was wet. It was terrible.

7.11
JOKE: What is a "term"?
A man told his doctor that he wasn't able to do all the things around the house that he used to do.
When the exam was complete, he said, "Now, Doc, I can take it. Tell me in plain English what is wrong with me."
"Well, in plain English," the doctor said, "you're just lazy."
"Okay," said the man. "Now give me the medical term so I can tell my wife."

7.12
READING: Subscribe to an internet e-letter and receive a new vocabulary lesson each week. www.englishtown.com
TO SUBSCRIBE: Go to www.englishtown.com/subscriptions and log in. Then click the newsletter you want and click update.

More Reading:
Visit these websites and learn about the local community—www.miami.com.
Click on TRAVEL AND VISITORS and then keep clicking to answer these questions

a) Look in Palm Beach: where is Dreher Park Zoo? When is it open?
b) Look at Miami-what is happening on South Beach? (new shows at the art galleries? When is the next festival?)
www.sunny.org
www.realcities.com (links to over 100 cities in the USA)
www.virtualkeywest.com

7.13
OPTIONAL
From Daniela: "Please, visit my new web page about my trip to Cancun."
www.geocities.com/danielapatruno/cancun.html
(Write some questions about her trip to Daniela at danibabe81@hotmail.com)
When did she go? What amazing animal did she touch?
What was she celebrating?

7.14
JOKE
An artist asked the gallery owner if there had been any interest in his paintings on display at that time.
"I have good news and bad news," the owner replied. "The good news is that a gentleman enquired about your work and wondered if it would appreciate in value after your death.
When I told him it would, he bought all 15 of your paintings."
"That's wonderful!" the artist exclaimed. "What's the bad news?"
"The guy was your doctor."

7.15
WRITE A DIALOG

Part A: Choose one of these situations and imagine the words that are said. Work with your partner.

Part B: Create another situation. Describe the situation and (if you want to) send it by e-mail to englishlesson@mail.com.

Immigration

a. "My sister wants to come to visit me. She wants to move here and get a job. Do you know a good attorney?" (you can recommend Jeff Campion at 764-6779, campionj@hotmail.com or www.campion-law.com)

b. Think of a conversation that you might have about immigration. Ralph asks you, "Why are you here? What visa did you use to come here?"

Situation # 7 (Immigration)

Luisa is studying English with a student visa, but it'll expire the next month. What can she do? Does she have to come back to her country to renew it? She talked with Mari, and Mari explained everything to her…..Write a conversation between Luisa and Mari!

7.16

Interlude

PAIRWORK or HOMEWORK

ANSWER THESE QUESTIONS

What is it like to move to South Florida?

What is different in South Florida (compared to your home city)?

What is similar?

Find a person who moved to South Florida. Write five questions that you want to ask the person.

1.

2.

3.

4.

5.

Write a composition using the answers from the interview. (You might want to tape record or videotape the answers so you can listen carefully to the words.)

Now read this interview that a student in the Nova ESL Program. Look for errors.

Mari was born in New York, and she graduated high school over there. She lived with her parents and her little brother in a pretty big apartment on the 14th floor of a huge building in the city. She was 16 years old when her father decided to come to Florida for vacations, and they ended up staying here to live. Here is her opinion about some things that she found different when she came here.

The Weather: It's hotter here, also I came in July, so it was the beginning of the summer.

The Places: She said that they had a lot of commercial places near their building; anyone could go walking to the supermarket to buy food, or to the drug store, etc. There isn't an area for houses or for residential or commercial buildings, everything is mixed. She also said that she thinks there are more things to do in New York than in Florida…she means amusement, restaurants, and parks. She says that since everything is near, the children and teenagers have more opportunities to enjoy the amusement places, because they can go on foot or on bike. She says that she was shocked when she came here, because everything was far, and there weren't too many places to have fun.

The Accent: She says that the native people of New York have a heavy accent, and it's very easy to notice it if you speak fluent English.

The Safety: She says that New York isn't any more dangerous than Florida…you're safe in both places…of course that there are some areas that are dangerous, like in Florida, but it's just as safe in both places.

The Transportation: Mari says that the public transportation is very common in New York….the taxis and the buses. She said that some people don't have a car, they only depend on public transportation. Because of that, there is a lot of noise on the streets…..that's another thing that she noticed when she came here: that everything was quiet. She also said, that here the traffic is terrible, because there is a lot of cars, and she says that over there, the traffic lights are coordinated, and when one of them is green, all of them are green too, so that's a thing that helps the traffic. Another thing that helps the traffic-she says-is that as here the distances are far, each member of a family has to have a car, so there are more cars on the streets. And over there, as the distances are closer, the families have one or two cars per family, or maybe none at all, because they can use the public transportation; that reduces the traffic.

She also says that people over there drive so fast, but very well, so the cars insurance is cheaper than here. She thinks that here, in Florida, it's more expensive because that reason.

The Holidays: Mari and her family felt very bad on their first Thanksgiving and Christmas, because they weren't with the rest of their family. She told me that she has a really big family, because her parents have a lot of brothers and sisters.

The conclusion: She says that she left many friends in New York, and she would have never moved if she would had been older. She loves the life over there, and she hopes to come back to live, some day. I like a lot the life in New York. (Interview by Daniela Patruno, *danibabe81@hotmail.com*. You can write to the author of this article and ask more questions.)

Corrected Version
Mari was born in New York, and she graduated high school over there. She lived with her parents and her little brother in a pretty big apartment on the 14th floor of a huge building in the city. She was 16 years old when her father decided to come to Florida for vacations, and they ended up staying here to live. Here is her opinion about some things that she found different when she came here.

The Weather: It's hotter here, also I came in July, so it was the beginning of the summer.

The Places: She said that they had a lot of commercial places near their building; anyone could go walking to the supermarket to buy food, or to the drug store, etc. There isn't an area for houses or for residential or commercial buildings, since everything is mixed. She also said that she thinks there are more things to do in New York than in Florida…she means amusement, restaurants, and parks. She says that since everything is near, the children and teenagers have more opportunities to enjoy the amusement places, because they can go on foot or on bike. She says that she was shocked when she came here, because everything was far, and there weren't too many places to have fun.

The Accent: She says that the native people of New York have a heavy accent, and it's very easy to notice it if you speak fluent English.

The Safety: She says that New York isn't any more dangerous than Florida…you're safe in both places…of course that there are some areas that are dangerous, like in Florida, but it's just as safe in both places.

The Transportation: Mari says that the public transportation is very common in New York….the taxis and the buses. She said that some people don't have a car, they only depend on public transportation. Because of that, there is a lot of noise on the streets…..that's another thing that she noticed when she came here: that everything was quiet. She also said, that here the traffic is terrible, because there is a lot of cars, and she says that over there, the traffic lights are coordinated, and when one of them is green, all of them are green too, so that's a thing that helps the traffic. Another thing that helps reduce the traffic, she says, is that as here the distances are far, each member of a family has to have a car, so there are more cars on the streets. In New York, as the distances are closer, the families have one or two cars per family, or maybe none at all, because they can use the public transportation; that reduces the traffic.

She also says that people over there drive so fast, but very well, so the cars insurance is cheaper than here. She thinks that here, in Florida, it's more expensive because that reason.

The Holidays: Mari and her family felt very bad on their first Thanksgiving and Christmas, because they weren't with the rest of their family. She told me that she has a really big family, because her parents have a lot of brothers and sisters.

The conclusion: She says that she left many friends in New York, and she would never have moved if she had been older. She loves the life over there, and she hopes to go back to live there, some day. She says, "I like the life in New York a lot."

8. Work

There are photos for this chapter at *www.teacherstoteachers.com*, then click on "ESL BOOK" and click on "Chapter 8."

8.1
READING
The way to see the work and the attitude of the people about work, is different in each country. Here, in general, the people are very fast and automatic in his/her job, that is efficiency. In my country the people are not used to work, their priority is not to work, like the people here.

It's sad but it is the real story our governments have gotten the people used to not working. They have given to the population milk, bread, bags, etc. And it hasn't been as a good action, it has been for presidential campaigns.

The Venezuelans in general, don't like to work. They are very lazy, and when they work you can notice that they do it unwillingly. I'm not meaning that everybody is like that, but I'm talking about most of the people, and that is already too much.

Here, there is something that encourages the people to work, and that is the stable economy, which gives to the population the possibility to work and obtain things. The people want to work from when they are young, and the country offers it to them. In my country it is very difficult because the economy is so bad, and even though you work, you won't have all that you need to live well. I think, this is a problem that has political and economical roots. By danibabe81@hotmail.com

8.2
PAIR WORK (CONVERSATION): Here are some words that you need to know. Work with your partner and write a sentence with each word or phrase:

The Puritan work ethic
Time is (friendly, everywhere, money, many, no problem)
My door is always (closed, red, open, broken)

8.3
PAIRWORK: Work with your partner and answer these questions.
How do people work in your country?

Do you have questions about the work system in the USA?

What surprised you when you came to the USA about employees? About employers? About the attitudes that people have about work?

Describe a problem that you had in the USA.

What did you do?

Do you have any recommendations?

8.4
READING and DISCUSSION
Talk with your partner about these responses by ESL students:
How do people work in your country?

-Most of people work in an honestly and decent way, but some people demand some extra payment of money to do a work.

Do you have questions about the work system in the USA?
-What do I need to get any job being a foreign person?
-How can I get a social security number?

What surprised you when you came to the USA about employees? About the attitudes that people have to work?
-In this country, the most important is the productivity. If you aren't a productive person, you can lose your job very fast.
-People here work from 7:00 am. to 5:00 pm. They are very worker .
-Here you have a lot of opportunities to find a good job or just a job to earn enough money to live well.
-The people work a lot, they are always very worried about money. I think the people are very serious I their work, from they are young. They are very practice, like machines.

Describe a problem that you had in the USA. What did you do?
-I have had a long time waiting for a stable and permanent job in the USA, so I started learning English and getting some experience in my area.

Do you have any recommendations?
-Everybody works here……the time is very important, nobody lose time, because that means to lose money. Be practical and do everything good. Don't think about do something illegal, because you'll going to be in troubles.

8.5
ABBREVIATIONS:
What is 24/7? What does the abbreviation stand for?
9-to-5

CEO
ASAP
PDQ
ICQ
IM

For more abbreviations related to work, see the web site at www.teacherstoteacher.com and click on "ESL Book".

8.6

ADVICE: "It's a good idea to…"

IAGI to get direct deposit on your checks from work. It saves time and the employer usually likes it.

IAGI to arrive at work about 15 or 20 minutes before the work starts.

IAGI to carry a photocopy of your passport or your work permit with you in case someone stops you and asks to see identification (usually a police officer).

Write some more "It's a good idea" points here with your partner:

1.

2.

3.

8.7

INTERNET: "Here are some internet sites for you to visit to find more information."

(If you know about other web sites, please send a message to english-lesson@mail.com and we will consider adding your suggestion to our web site.)

www.boa.com

The Bank of America web site is full of useful information.

Visit this web site for more information that was submitted by students: www.geocities.com/talkinternational/work.html

A group of grammar quizzes
webster.commnet.edu/grammar/quiz_list.stm

Try to find a job: *www.hotjobs.com* or *www.monster.com.*

Visit this web site for more information that was submitted by students: www.geocities.com/talkinternational/fun.html

You can read about a business in Hawaii. Ask yourself some questions and then read the article at this internet web page:
www.geocities.com/steveinhawaii/icecream.html
What is the name of the owner of the ice cream store?
Where did he live before he moved to Hawaii?
How much is a cone of ice at Matsumoto's ice store?
What is the name of the ice cream store?
How many flavors does the store sell?

8.8
LETTER
"Write a letter to the manager of the bank to explain your problem. Ask for help with a bank wire. Inquire about the cost of sending money via a bank wire." (You need the money to pay for some products that your new company is importing.) Then show the letter to your teacher.

8.9
ANOTHER LETTER
Write your resume (you can see an example at www.geocities.com/talkinternational/resumeexample.html) and then

write a letter to go with the resume. Then show the letter to your teacher.

8.10

GRAMMAR

Watch the "only" in these sentences

What are the differences between the sentences.

A-Only the waiter can bring water to the table.

B-The water can only bring water to the table.

C-The waiter can bring only water to the table.

D-The waiter can bring water only to the table.

Discuss with your partner and then write your explanations of the differences. Show your sentences to your teacher.

8.11

PUNCTUATION PRACTICE

An English professor wrote the words, "Woman without her man is nothing," on the blackboard and directed the students to punctuate it correctly. (The answer is in section 8.13.) Try it: Woman without her man is nothing

8.12

VOCABULARY

We will look at the vocabulary used in e-mail communications.

1. TTFN is another way of saying hello. (True of False?)

2. If you want to wink, you can send a message that includes ;-) True or False?

3. If you receive a confusing e-mail, you could send this symbol: :-/ What does it mean?

4. When do you use BRB?

5. BFN means "buy fives newspapers" or "bye for now" or "Bring Food Now" (Choose one).

ANSWERS
1 Ta Ta For Now (Good bye)
2 A wink is when you close one eye. A blink is when you close both eyes.
3 :-/ shows your face is confused.
4 I will BE RIGHT BACK. (I will return soon.)
5 (good) Bye For Now

You can see more "etiquette for the Internet" by going to www.yahoo.com, then click on "check e-mail" and then look for "Take the Yahoo Mail Netiquette Quiz".

8.13
READING
Subscribe to an internet e-letter and receive a new vocabulary lesson each week. Subscribe to The Christian Science Monitor's print edition and get 31 issues FREE! www.csmonitor.com/subscribe

Here is a list of interesting facts that arrived one day by e-mail. Underline the words that you don't understand and ask the teacher to explain.

Models twenty years ago weighed 8% less than the average woman. Today they weigh 23% less.

Marilyn Monroe wore a size 14.

If Barbie were a real woman, she'd have to walk on all fours due to her proportions.

The average woman weighs 144 lbs and wears between a 12-14.

One out of every four college aged women has an eating disorder.

The models in the magazines are airbrushed-not perfect!

A psychological study in 1995 found that three minutes spent looking at a fashion magazine caused 70% of women to feel depressed, guilty, and shameful.

An English professor wrote the words, "Woman without her man is nothing," on the blackboard and directed the students to punctuate it correctly.
The men wrote: "Woman, without her man, is nothing
The women wrote: Woman! Without her, man is nothing.

8.14
WORKSHEETS
Idioms, Proverbs, Phrasal verbs
Visit this web site for idioms about work that Roxana submitted:
www.geocities.com/talkinternational/roxanajobs.html

8.15
WRITE A DIALOG
Part A: Choose one of these situations and imagine the words that are said. Work with your partner.
Part B: Create another situation. Describe the situation and (if you want to) send it by e-mail to englishlesson@mail.com.

Work

a. Jorge Martinez (your neighbor's son) wants to get a job delivering newspapers. He wants you to be a reference for him. A person from the newspaper company calls you.

b. Mrs. Martinez wants you to help her son find a job. You are happy because Jorge has been spending his time after school spitting watermelon seeds onto your garden. You want him to find a job. Use a newspaper to look for a good job for Jorge. (More homework: call the job and ask for more information about the job, such as working hours and the location, salary, etc.)

Situation # 8 (Work)

Danny is a lawyer, who graduated from law school in his country. He already did the final exam to become a lawyer in Florida, but he doesn't know how to find a job in his area. What is best for him? He called one of his friends who is a lawyer here. What did he tell our friend Danny? Write about it!

9. Education

There are photos for this chapter at *www.teacherstoteachers.com*, then click on "ESL BOOK" and click on "Chapter 9."

9.1
READING
The educational system in Venezuela is fairly different that the system here in the USA. Firstly, we have to do 3 years of preschool, 6 years of primary and 5 years of basic and diversified education (those are the names). A child enter preschool when she/he is 4 years old, and they enter primary when they are 7 years old. I don't have knowledge about the ages to study here, but I think they should be the same or similar.

We have private and public schools in Venezuela, but only the private ones serve, because the government doesn't pay to the public schools' teachers, so they don't work, and the classes are interrupted for a week or more time, each month. It's a terrible problem, because that people cannot pay a private school, and the children are the ones who suffer the main damage. Because they cannot study, they look for other activities which almost always are bad. Well, that's the problem with the public schools. I think here, in the USA, there are not these kinds of problems, the public schools are good, and everybody goes there.

On other hand, in Venezuela, during the school season, you can't choose subjects. We don't have optional subjects as here. But the last two years of "high-school" you have to do it at "sciences" or at "humanities". With sciences, you take chemical, physical, math, biology, earth's science, etc., and with humanities you take French, Latin, sociology, literature, art, psychology, etc. Both branch are interesting but you have to choose only one to study.

Another important difference is the way to enter the universities. In Venezuela, there are really few good universities, so they are very strict with the admissions. There is one important test, like the Toefl, that the students have to take, it has the same format of the Toefl. That's only one requirement for all the universities, and its name is "CNU", everybody knows about CNU, as here the people know about the Toefl. After that, you have to take the faculty intern's test, and it depends on how many quotas there are available, if you enter or not....it depends on the position that your test is, with respect to the others.

Most of the universities courses last 5 years, and the quality of the teachers is excellent......of almost everybody. We don't use credits, as here, we have to do the 5 years of the course, and if you pass everything, you'll graduate.

I think the quality of the private schools and of the universities, is very good in my country....the only problem we have it with the public schools, and it's a really big problem because we need more trained people to improve our country.

9.2
PAIR WORK (CONVERSATION)
Here are some words that you need to know. Work with your partner and write a sentence with each word or phrase:
School
High School
University
Student Loan (see Finance)

9.3

PAIRWORK: Work with your partner and answer these questions.

Describe the educational system in your country.

Do you have questions about the school system in the USA?

What surprised you when you came to the USA about schools and teachers?

Describe a problem that you had in the USA.

What did you do?

Do you have any recommendations?

9.4

READING and DISCUSSION

Talk with your partner about these responses by ESL students:

Describe the educational system in your country.

-In Venezuela, we have 6 years of primary and 5 years of "bachiller-ato" or secondary; which involve 3 years of basic and the last two years are "diversify". The university is the superior education, and it regularly takes 5 years per course.

-In Korea not all the people can go to the school, because it is very expensive.

-In Colombia we study in private schools because they are better than the public's ones.

-In Dominican Republic, the E.S is maternal (K-PK). Primary (1-6th grade). Intermediate (7-8th grade), High School, and university.

Do you have questions about the school system in the USA?

-Do you have to do any research essay to graduate high school?

-How many letters do you have to qualify?

-How do you get an I-20 form?

-How can I do to get in some university?

What surprised you when you came to the USA about schools and teachers?

-The teachers are informal. There isn't too much protocol with the classes and they are near to the students. There is respect to both sides, but there is more confidence between each other.

-The USA gives a lot of opportunities to study for everybody. There are public schools, sports, etc.

-The intensity is stronger in Colombia.

-The Colombian students are more responsible.

-Sports are more important in the USA.

-There are more opportunities available in the USA.

-The college education is separated of the university and some schools.

Do you have any recommendations?

-If you want to study in a university here, the first thing that you have to do, is to take the TOEFL, and each university asks you for a minimum qualification to get in. It's usually between 500 and 700 points. After you take the TOEFL and you pass it, you have to translate your qualifications to here's system....There are some companies that do it here. Then, you have to present all your papers in the faculty of your preference, to fill in the inscription form, and to pay the fee.

-If you practice some sport in your country, and you want to study without leaving your sport, this is the correct country. Also, you have a grant if you are a good sporty.

9.5
ABBREVIATIONS
What is UF? What does the abbreviation stand for?
UCLA
NYU
TESOL
TESL

TEFL
TOEFL
Can you think of other abbreviations for universities?

9.6
ADVICE
"It's a good idea to…"
IAGI to talk with advisors at a school. Some people are lazy in the USA, so don't be afraid to talk to many people to ask for advice.
IAGI to tell other people about the advice that you already learned. Then they can say "Oh, that's right" or "Well, here's some more information that you need to consider." It will save time for the second and third person that you talk with.

9.7
INTERNET
"Here are some internet sites for you to visit to find more information." (If you know about other web sites, please send a message to englishlesson@mail.com and we will consider adding your suggestion to our web site.)

A good ESL site
www.eslpr.com Puerto Rico
This site claims to have two million students: www.epals.com

Visit this web site for more information that was submitted by students: www.geocities.com/talkinternational/education.html

What to give to those who have everything? Give the gift of words. Here is a gift that keeps on giving. To enter a gift subscription of A.Word.A.Day, please visit wordsmith.org/awad/gift.html or ask them to subscribe themselves at wordsmith.org/awad/subscribe.html

Here's an example of what you will receive when you subscribe:
timorous (TIM-uhr-uhs) adjective, full of fear, timid. [Middle English, from Middle French timoureus, from Medieval Latin timorosus, from Latin timor fear, from timere, to fear.]

9.8
LETTER
"Write a letter to the director of a school and explain your problem. Ask for something. Ask for help." Then show the letter to your teacher.

9.9
LISTENING
On the CD-1, available from www.teacherstoteachers.com, you can listen to the conversation. With your partner, listen to ten sentences, write down the entire sentences and then show the sentences to your teacher.

9.10
OPTIONAL Listening and Pronunciation Exercise
Call 1-800-555-TELL. The free call connects you to dozens of interesting sources of information. It works with your voice, so you need to speak clearly. It's a good practice of your pronunciation and your listening.

For example: After the voice says, "Welcome to Tell Me," you can say "Weather" and the system switches to give you information about the weather. You can interrupt the recording by saying "MAIN MENU" or you can say any of these categories:
Restaurants
Movies

Driving directions
Taxi
Weather
Time
News
Sports
Please try it today! It is a good exercise for your pronunciation and listening!

9.11
GRAMMAR
Fill in the blanks below. CAN YOU IMPROVE THESE SENTENCES?

I want to know the _____. (true, truth)

I want to know the _____ story. (true, truth)

What is the opposite of "true"? The opposite of "truth"?
He told me a _____ story.

Who, whose, it, its, it's
Write a sentence for each of these words. Ask your teacher to look at your sentences.

9.12
READING
Subscribe to an internet e-letter and receive a new vocabulary lesson each week. Go to *www.esl.about.com*. Click on the area that reads: "Stay up-to-date! Subscribe to our newsletter." And put in your e-mail address. You'll start receiving a weekly letter by e-mail.

9.13
WRITE A DIALOG
Part A: Choose one of these situations and imagine the words that are said. Work with your partner.
Part B: Create another situation. Describe the situation and (if you want to) send it by e-mail to englishlesson@mail.com.

Education
a. Mrs. Martinez wants to talk a course of English but she is too frightened to go alone to the school. She asks you to come with her to translate.
b. Jorge wants to go to the local university. Mrs. Martinez wants you to help translate the interview. Use words like "transcript," "financial aid" and "I-20."

Situation # 9 (Education)
Karla wants to study medicine at Nova......she already knows English, but she doesn't know where can she take the TOEFL. Where can she translate her qualifications? What else does she need? How much does it cost? What is the cost? Which are the credit plans or what loans are available for the foreign students here? She called Orlando by phone, because he is studying business and administration at Nova. What did he tell her?

ANSWERS
The first composition needs several corrections.

The educational system in Venezuela is fairly different that [1] the system here in the USA. Firstly, we have to do 3 years of preschool, 6 years of primary and 5 years of basic and diversified education (those are the names). A child enter preschool when she/he is 4 years old, and they enter primary when they are 7 years old. I don't have knowledge about the ages to study here, but I think they should be the same or similar.

[1] it is different than the system in the USA. In Spanish "que" can be THAN or THAT:
Ese es el carro que vi ayer. (that)
This is the car that I saw yesterday.
Su carro es mas pequeno que el carro de ella. (than)
His car is smaller than her car.

We have private and public schools in Venezuela, but only the private ones serve, because the government doesn't pay to the public schools' teachers, so they don't work, and the classes are interrupted for a week or more time, each month. It's a terrible problem, because that people cannot pay a private school, and the children are the ones who suffer the main damage. Because they cannot study, they look for other activities which almost always are bad. Well, that's the problem with the public schools. I think here, in the USA, there are not these kinds of problems, the public schools are good, and everybody goes there.

On other hand [*], in Venezuela, during the school season, you can't choose subjects. We don't have optional subjects as here [see 1 below]. But the last two years of "high-school" you have to do it at "sciences" or at "humanities". With sciences, you take chemical, physical, math, biology, earth's science, etc., and with humanities you take French, Latin, sociology, literature, art, psychology, etc. Both branch are interesting but you have to choose only one to study.
[*] = on the other hand

Another important difference is the way to enter the universities. In Venezuela, there are really few good universities, so they are very strict with the admissions. There is one important test, like the Toefl, that the students have to take, it has the same format of the Toefl. That's only one requirement for all the universities, and its name is "CNU", everybody knows about CNU, as here the people know about the Toefl. After that, you have to take the faculty intern's test, and it depends on how many quotas there are available, if you enter or not....it depends on the position that your test is, with respect to the others.

Most of the universities courses last 5 years, and the quality of the teachers is excellent......of almost everybody. We don't use credits, as here [1], [2]we have to do the 5 years of the course, and if you pass everything, you'll graduate.

I think the quality of the private schools and of the universities, is very good in my country. The only problem we have it with the public schools, and it's a really big problem because we need more trained people to improve our country.

[1] = We don't use credits, like here.
[2] = We have to do the five years of the course and if you pass everything you will graduate. [change a comma to a period]

If you are not interested in immigration laws (which are connected to education), please skip this section and go directly to Chapter 10.

Information about Immigration (prepared especially for students)
The following pages are provided as a public service by Jeff Campion, an attorney in Fort Lauderdale. www.campionlaw.com/. Consult an attorney if you have specific questions. (Jeffrey E. Campion, 644 SE 4th Avenue, Fort Lauderdale, FL 33301, 954 764 6779, fax 954 764 6789, campionj@hotmail.com)

These are some basic questions that students might have:
Can I work in the US as a student?
The answer is "possibly." A foreigner may work without INS approval if it is on-campus or curricular employment. On-campus employment means working for the school you are currently attending. The rule of thumb, the school must use is "Has the position traditionally been

filled by a student?" If so, the school may hire a student. At the same time if the employment is as a result of scholarship, fellowship, etc., a foreigner may work as well and there is no need for prior INS authorization.

With respect to Curriculum employment, if the foreigner's course of study requires that he be employed for experience in the field, then employment is possible without INS authorization. However, the foreigner must first be a student for 9 months before accepting the curriculum employment.

The INS also allows foreign students to work after INS approval if there is an unforeseen economic necessity or if it is for practical training. With respect to unforeseen economic necessity, there must be a severe economic hardship caused by unforeseen circumstance beyond the student's control, the foreigner must have been an F-1 for one year, the foreigner must obtain a recommendation from the school and there must be INS approval.

Practical training for F-1 students is available pre-graduation and post-graduation. A student may work during vacation or during the school year (not to exceed 20 hours a week). Post-graduation practical training is also available after all the course requirements for the degree have been completed or when the course of study is completed. However, to qualify, the student must have been an F-1 for nine months. But the job cannot last more than 12 months. Lastly, practical training is not permitted for students who are studying language.

If the foreign student wants to work after graduation, he may either use the practical training (as mentioned above) or request a work visa from the INS. The INS grants, generally, three types of work visas that most aliens attempt to obtain: E1/E2, H-1B and L-1A.

E1/E2

The E visa is used for nationals of a country (which is the same as the investing company) that has a treaty with the US involving trade and/or investment. (Unless it is a foreigner personally doing the investment.) Then the foreigner would qualify. The distinction in the visas depends on whether the US company will be doing trade or investment.

If the US company will be doing trade, then it must be substantial, principally between the US and the home country. If the US company will be investing in the US to provide goods or services in the US, then the investment must be active, substantial and create jobs. There is no limit to the number of E visas granted each year and, although they must be renewed every two years, there is no limit to the number of renewals.

H-1B
The H-1B visa is for a foreigner in a specialty occupation. This means that the foreigner has at least a bachelor's degree or its equivalent. The INS allows a foreigner to use three years experience for one year of college, satisfying the bachelor's degree requirement with 12 years of experience. There is a limit on the number of visas issued each year, and they are normally used up by April each year.

L-1A Visa
The L-1A is the preferred visa because it avoids one of the two steps to residency known as "Labor Certification," which can add another two years on to the residency process. In order to qualify for an L-1A, the foreigner must have worked for at least one year of the last three years for a foreign company as a manager or executive. The Foreign Company must have a relationship with a Florida company (parent, subsidiary, sister or affiliate. The rules can become somewhat complex, but as long as the Foreign Company own 51% of the Florida Company there should be no problems. The Foreign Company then transfers the foreigner to the US on an L-1A visa. Both businesses must provide

goods or services and continue to do so for the entire time the foreigner is on the L-1A.

Social Security Card
If a foreigner desires a SS card, he must have previous work authorization from the INS or be a resident.

Residency (The Green Card)
A person may become a resident through a family relationship or a job. The relationships that allow for immigration are
1) immediate relative of US citizen (spouse, children, parents) for which there is no limit on the number of visas and
2) other close family of citizen or resident, such as unmarried children of the citizen (over 21), married children, spouses and unmarried children of residents, brothers and sisters of citizens.

Each subcategory of the second category has special requirements and varying waiting times for a Green Card. TO become a resident under either category, you must go through the same steps as detailed below.

Employment Based Immigration
Generally there are three steps to Green Card approval: labor certification, a permanent resident application and adjustment of status.
Labor Certification: The Department of Labor ensures that the foreigner will not take a US worker's position. While this is a difficult process, it is done with regularity. A labor certification is not needed with family based immigration or if the foreigner would qualify for an L-1A visa. After it is approved, a permanent residence application can be filed.
Permanent Resident Petition: The second step requires making an application to INS requesting that the foreigner be classified as eligible to immigrate under the Immigration and Nationality Act. A separate labor certification is not required for someone that has an L-1A visa, but it is required for those foreigners that attempt to pursue residency

and qualify only for an H-1B or E visa. Once approved, a Visa Priority Date is given. This date is important, as there is a limited number of Green Cards issued each year. Once Green Cards become available, they will be issued in order of this priority date.

Adjustment of Status: when the permanent residence petition has been approved, an application to adjust status to permanent resident will be filed. (A foreigner could choose to return to his home country and request the Green Card form the US consulate located there, but my experience has been that most people prefer to stay in the US.) When approved, the foreigner will be required to attend an interview for his adjustment of status and to obtain his card. At that meeting he will need to bring his passport and a picture ID. The time needed from receipt of notice of approval to the completion of the interview in step iii can take between 12 and 18 months.

An Expired I-94: If a foreigner remains in the US after the I-94 expires, there are several consequences. He may not be permitted to obtain residency in the US by adjusting status (step iii). The foreigner may have to go to the US consulate located in his country for the Green Card. He might not be permitted to re-enter the US for up to 10 years if he leaves.

If the foreigner remains in the US for 180 days after the I-94 expires and leaves, he will be prohibited from returning for three years. If he remains in the US for one year after the I-94 expires and leaves, he will be prohibited from returned for 10 years. Clearly, there are severe consequences for remaining in the US after the I-94 expires.

Conclusion: A foreign student can work here while studying. After studying, he can work in the US with INS authorization. He can receive a SS card only if he has INS work authorization. He can become a resident through a family relationship or through work. Remaining here after the I-94 expires has serious consequences.

10. Fun

There are photos for this chapter at *www.teacherstoteachers.com*, then click on "ESL BOOK" and click on "Chapter 10."

10.1
READING
In Florida you can find a lot of fun; there are a lot of restaurants, amusement parks, and many others places where you can enjoy with your family and friends.

To summarize, you have in Orlando, MGM, Epcot Center, Universal Studios and Sea Word…..In Tampa, you have Busch Gardens and Adventure Island, with amazing roller coasters. Here, in South Florida, you can find the Grand Prix Race-O-Rama with a fabulous Sky Coaster, miniature golf, go-carts racing, and meny others attractions.

In addition, you can find fairly good restaurants, like "Tarantella" in Weston, Ft. Lauderdale, with Italian food. "La Torreta", in Weston, and in Davie, with pizzas. "Tony Roma's" in Collins Avenue and in other places with pork ribs as a specialty.

There is also a unique restaurant called Dave and Buster's, where you can eat, you can play in interactive games, and also there are billiards…..it's very, very fun.

Another entertainment that you have here, are the Everglades Holiday Park; you have airboats tours, fishing, boat rentals, campground, etc.

In respect to cinemas, there are several of them here, but I only know one in Sheridan: "Muvico", with 24 movie rooms and the best movies.

Well, I think in Florida there are a lot of fun and thinks to do, just be careful with the children and don't miss to jump into the "Sky Coaster" in Grand Prix Race-O-Rama.

10.2
PAIR WORK (CONVERSATION)
Here are some words that you need to know. Work with your partner and write a sentence with each word or phrase:
Restaurants
Vacation
Amusement parks
Tips (propinas)

10.3
PAIRWORK
Work with your partner and answer these questions.
Your brother's employer is visiting South Florida with his family. Your brother asked you to make some recommendations for
a great restaurant near the beach…
a good zoo…
a good restaurant in Miami…
a place to take children somewhere in South Florida…it might rain so the place must be covered.
What surprised you when you came to the USA about restaurants / movie theaters / clubs / amusement parks?

Describe a problem that you had in the USA. What did you do?

Do you have any recommendations?

10.4
READING and DISCUSSION
Talk with your partner about these responses by ESL students:

Look for the errors
A great restaurant near the beach…
-Crab house
-"A la Pasta con Porcel". Restaurant at 270 Collins av. Miami Beach, Fl. Italian and international cuisine.
-MAI-KAI. It's a Polynesian restaurant.

A good zoo….
-The metro zoo that houses more than 700 wild animals in a cage less environment and it's one of the best of the world's great zoos.

A good restaurant in Miami….
-Los Ranchos
-Aerosquadron. In 836.

A place to take children somewhere in South Florida…
-Seaquarium
-Magic Puppets.
-Chuckie-cheese.

What surprised you when you came to the USA about restaurants/movie theaters/clubs/amusement parks?
-The parks are big and attractive.
-The people is very ordered.

Describe a problem that you had in the USA. What did you do?
-Someone stole my kid's bicycle in a park, and I had to call the Administration and they told me that I had to call the police.
-I was a child, and I was in MGM with my parents......thee were a lot of people and I got lost. It was terrible, I was like 6 years old, and I was alone in the park. Finally, my parents found me. They were desperate, and they bought me one of those rapes like a phone cable to keeping m with them.

Do you have any recommendations?
Keep your children with you in the parks, because they are exciting with the attractions and they don't realize of anything…..there are many people, and it's so easy to lose the children.

10.5
ABBREVIATIONS
What is TGIF? What does the abbreviation stand for?
MOMA
MOA
RBI (baseball)
PAT (football)

10.6
ADVICE
"It's a good idea to…" IAGI
IAGI to ask one person in your group to avoid drinking alcohol. This will be the person who will drive everyone home (the designated driver)
IAGI to go for a walk after a big meal. The digestion is helped with a little movement. Remember to bring a list of jokes so that people will laugh (laughing is also good for digestion).

10.7
INTERNET
"Here are some internet sites for you to visit to find more information."

(If you know about other web sites, please send a message to english-lesson@mail.com and we will consider adding your suggestion to our web site.)

bali-paradise.com/see-bali/index.html
The Bali site is full of useful information about this tropical island that Steve visited in 1998. He hopes to return there some day. You can write to Steve at englishlesson@mail.com and ask him questions about what you read about in this web site.

www.angelfire.com/biz2/wayanmerta/
Steve created this web site for his friend Wayan Merta. Visit it and then ask Steve som2222e questions.

www.geocities.com/punchbuggyclub/index.html
Learn about the Punch Buggy Club. Then learn about the teaching program in Peru (which is supported by the Punch Buggy Club). Yes, this is fun!

Visit this web site for more information that was submitted by students: www.geocities.com/talkinternational/fun.html

10.9
LETTER
"Write a letter to the marketing person of a visitors office. Tell him or her about the city. You can see an example at www.teacherstoteachers.com and then click on "Fort Lauderdale Book." Write a letter that describes the good things about your favorite city. And, if you have

time, write a letter to Rudi Huber (his address is below) to tell him what you think about Fort Lauderdale.

Go to www.teacherstoteachers.com and hit "Fort Lauderdale BOOK" and you will see pages from a book that was inspired by reading the following composition…

A city I love
No question: Fort Lauderdale. This is also a reason why I'm here again. I prefer towns with nice skies, a colorful lifestyle, with a town of class and fun.

Another advantage: The green zones in the middle of the city. And don't forget the canals and the harbors with the nice boats.

The absolute highlight: Las Olas Boulevard, with all the nice stores and restaurants. Then Fort Lauderdale is an excellent point to start for trips to famous places like Miami, West Palm Beach the Keys and a lot of other destinations.

In April 2000 I was here in Fort Lauderdale for the first time. A friend of mine lives six months of the year in Port Charlotte near Fort Myers, and he invites me last spring to visit this really beautiful state. We started our Florida sightseeing tour here in Fort Lauderdale and at the end of the trip I knew it: I'll come back to Lauderdale. Now I'm here. This time is not to go on vacation. The reason is to brush up. no, improve my English.

But I'm sure I'll not only be in the school. No, I will go to the own and all its beautiful places. Because Fort Lauderdale is a city I love.
Rudi Huber, rudhuber@aol.com

OPTIONAL PAIR WORK

Work with your partner and create a letter. Write to Rudi and ask him more questions.

10.10
LISTENING
On the CD-1, available from www.teacherstoteachers.com, you can listen to the conversation. With your partner, listen to ten sentences, write down the entire sentences and then show the sentences to your teacher.

10.11
GRAMMAR
fill in the blank: He is a _____ man. His business is _____. He is a s_____. He doesn't want to _____ (fail, failure, failing, unlucky,).

Put these words in the blanks below: I, my, me, she, her, us, we, our
Janet and _____ went to the Sawgrass Mall. A stupid shopper ran into _____ and knocked both of _____ on the ground. I stood up and asked, "What are you doing?" The shopper said, "I'm sorry," and then ran away.

Janet picked up _____ purse and said, "That shopper should be more careful."

Then another shopper bumped into Janet and _____. I saw the second person reach into Janet's bag. "Look out! Thief!" I shouted. We pushed away from the shopper and then we reported that person to the local security guard. We were breathing very hard. "This is not _____ day!" Janet said.

10.12
VOCABULARY

Imagine that you are visiting Publix Supermarket. On the cart is a list of categories. Work with your partner. Try to match the product with the right category and row (aisle).

Categories (you can also call the row "aisle"-ask your teacher to check your pronunciation: "a-iil"). If you don't understand the category, ask your teacher.
Candy (row 5)
Dietetic Foods (row 2)
Pet foods (row 8)
Beverages (row 9)
Juices, Canned (row 2)
Detergents (row 7)
Meats, canned (row 3)
Fruits, dried (row 2)
Ethnic foods (row 3)
Vegetables, frozen (row 14)
Health foods (row 7)
Cereals (row 6)
Household supplies (row 8)
Disinfectants (row 7)

Products (some of the products are very popular and many customers know the name of the product better than the category)
Weight Watchers Low-Calorie Apple Snacks
Bottled water
A 2-liter bottle of soda
Orange juice in a can.
Dishwashing soap
Taco shells
Grits
Oatmeal
Brooms
Mop

Special K
Spam
Sponge
Raisins
Ammonia
Raisin Bran
Cascade
Lysol spray
Rice noodle soup (for the microwave oven)
Windex
Frozen green beans

More activities: Your partner is a customer who is looking for something. You are the manager of the store. Your partner asks for Orange Juice. You say, "Canned Juice is on Aisle 2" (use the numbers in the categories above).

10.13
READING
Subscribe to an internet e-letter and receive a new vocabulary lesson each week.

FUN PLACES TO VISIT
www.miami.com
www.sunny.org (Fort Lauderdale)
www.realcities.com (cities around the USA)
In Fort Lauderdale, visit the Port Everglades Building at 1800 Eller Drive. Park in the parking lot and walk around the building. There is a picnic table on the lawn. Do NOT FEED THE MANATEES.

www.miamiseaquarium.com Miami Seaquarium's website (more information about manatees) and pictures of manatees that have been saved by the staff.

Homosassa Springs State Park is a wonderful place to see manatees. (352) 628-5343, or write to HSSP, 4150 S. Suncoast Blvd., Homosassa, FL 34446.

Save the Manatee Club, 1-800-432-JOIN

Manatee Survival Foundation, 954-943-4391 (You can request a slide show without charge, plus manatee trading cards and other educational materials.)

Blue Spring State Park, 2100 West French Avenue, Orange City, FL, 904-775-3663
www.dep.state.fl.us/parks and look for Blue Spring.

10.14
WRITE A DIALOG
Part A: Choose one of these situations and imagine the words that are said. Work with your partner.
Part B: Create another situation. Describe the situation and (if you want to) send it by e-mail to englishlesson@mail.com.

Fun
a. A person comes to your door and knocks. "Hi, I'm new to the area. My name is Fred Jones. I just moved here from California. I want to take my boss to dinner and I don't know the restaurants in town. Can you give me some suggestions?"
b. Fred Jones also wants to know about a good place to stay in Orlando.
c. Fred Jones wants to visit some cities in Florida (Key west, Tampa, Cocoa, etc.) Give him some suggestions.
d. You are at the movies. You are buying popcorn and you see a neighbor. Start a conversation.

e. You are at the movie theater. You are buying popcorn. Suddenly you hear a crash. You turn and you see soda and popcorn on the floor. Jorge was not looking and he hit an old man. He dropped the soda and popcorn. Mrs. Martinez is very sorry and she sees you. "Can you help me? I can't talk to this man that Jorge bumped into. I want to say I'm sorry."

Situation # 10 (Fun)
Roberto went to a restaurant last week and he ordered a great dish……well…..great by its name!! Because he didn't know how was it was made or what the ingredients were. He asked the waitress, and she told him about the whole preparation of the dish and all the ingredients that it had. Poor Roberto didn't understand anything, and then, he didn't like the meal. Write a conversation between Roberto and the waitress!

ANSWERS
The Composition
In Florida you can find a lot of fun. There are a lot of restaurants, amusement parks, and many others places where you can enjoy with your family and friends.
To summarize, you have in Orlando, MGM, Epcot Center, Universal Studios and Sea Word…..In Tampa, you have Busch Gardens and Adventure Island, with amazing roller coasters. Here, in South Florida, you can find the Grand Prix Race-O-Rama with a fabulous Sky Coaster, miniature golf, go-carts racing, and many others attractions.
In addition, you can find fairly good restaurants, like "Tarantella" in Weston, Ft. Lauderdale, with Italian food. "La Torreta", in Weston, and in Davie, with pizzas. "Tony Roma's", on Collins Avenue and in other places with pork ribs as a specialty.

There is also a unique restaurant called Dave and Buster's, where you can eat, you can play in interactive games, and also there are billiards...it's very, very fun.

11. Communication

There are photos for this chapter at *www.teacherstoteachers.com*, then click on "ESL BOOK" and click on "Chapter 11".

11.1
READING
Nowadays, the first mass media in the whole world is, without doubt, internet. This is the most important technological advance that the human being has done. And it's really amazing how it has developed in a very short time.

This is something that anybody would have imagined 20 or 10 years ago…. all the world is connected by internet, you can communicate with any person in everywhere by a local call, you can buy whatever you want in the virtual stores, you can advertise your product or enterprise thru a web page, and everybody in the world have access to it. You can obtain software, you can see and talk with people everywhere, you can take a tour and look beautiful landscapes with animation and movement of amazing places, you can find all the information that you want about any topic, you can find photos, etc.

The advantages of Internet are infinite and I think they are going to increase with the pass of the time. Internet is, practically, a new thing, and it allows us many things, as I mentioned before. One of the things is the free trade of everything; you can buy, sell, advertise, download music by free, etc. And all those transactions need to be legalized, so in the future it will have "internet lawyers" and a "internet constitution".

Every day it's more important the communication and the things that we do by internet, and I think it's going to provide job for million of people of any profession…more than what it's providing now.
(Go to the end of the chapter to see the corrections.)

11.2
PAIR WORK (CONVERSATION)
Here are some words that you need to know. Work with your partner and write a sentence with each word or phrase:
Internet
TV
Telephone
Mail
Radio

11.3
PAIRWORK
Work with your partner and answer these questions.
How do people get news in your country?
Do you have questions about the media system in the USA?
What surprised you when you came to the USA about the TV news?
About the newspapers?
Describe a problem that you had in the USA.
What did you do?
Do you have any recommendations?

11.4
READING and DISCUSSION
Talk with your partner about these responses by ESL students:
Look for the errors

How do people get news in your country?
Most of the news, the people get it by the different newspapers. Some people don't buy the newspaper and they get news by TV or by radio.

Do you have questions about the media system in the USA? How many suppliers of phone service and internet service do the USA have? And which ones are they?

Which one is a good radio station here?

What surprised you when you came to the USA about the TV news? About the newspapers?
About the newspaper, I was surprised that there is more advertising than news…..in major of them.

Describe a problem that you had in the USA.
When I came here….the first time that I tried to call somebody by phone, I didn't know when I had to dial "1" or "954" or "305" before the number. It was confusing to me, and every time I heard that dumb message: "I'm sorry, you don't have to dial……."

What did you do?
I asked somebody, and he explained to me that Miami code was 305, and Fort Lauderdale code was 954. And he told me that I had to dial 1-954 if I'm in Miami and I'm calling to Fort Lauderdale……1-305 if I'm calling from Fort Lauderdale to Miami. Just 305 if I'm calling to Miami from Miami. And just the
number if I'm calling to Ft. Lauderdale from there same. Those codes have to be dialed before the number with which you want linking.

Do you have any recommendations?
-Dial this code before the number

Code	to	from
1-954	Ft. Lauderdale	Miami
1-305	Miami	Ft. Lauderdale
305	Miami	Miami
954 or 754	Ft. Lauderdale	Ft. Lauderdale

There is a new area code (754) that started on January 2002. People will need to learn that, when they call from one part of Fort Lauderdale to another part of Fort Lauderdale, they will need to add three digits. The number for TALK school will be 954.565.8505 (you need to add 954 before the usual 7 digits).

-Don't watch too much TV……..the programs here absorb too much time the people, and they don't do anything else.
-Don't buy a free computer in exchange of an internet subscription with a contrite of three years….because it is coming a free internet supplier, and the companies now, are trying to tie the people by three years paying them, just giving them a "free" computer. At the end, you will pay them more than the real
price of the computer.

11.5
ABBREVIATIONS
What is URL? What does the abbreviation stand for?
KSC
NASA
DOD
EVA
GMT
JPL
RAM
ROM
G (20 G hard drive)

M (333 M Hertz, the speed of the computer)
K (128 K RAM)
The answers are at the end of the chapter. You can find more abbreviations at the ESL BOOK web site (click on Chapter 11).

11.6
ADVICE: "It's a good idea to…"
…visit the post office in the late morning (10-11 am) or early afternoon (2-3 pm).
…visit the main post office after 7 p.m. because there is a late pick up around 8:30 p.m.
…call ahead before going to a store to see if the product is in the store. Can you and your partner think of other good ideas? Send them to *englishlesson@mail.com*.

11.7
INTERNET
"Here are some internet sites for you to visit to find more information." (If you know about other web sites, please send a message to englishlesson@mail.com and we will consider adding your suggestion to our web site.)

Visit this web site for more information that was submitted by students: www.geocities.com/talkinternational/communication.html

www.usps.com
The US Postal Service has a website where you can buy stamps on line and get questions answered.

www.herald.com (the Miami Herald's web site)

www.sun-sentinel.com

www.nbc6.net (the web site of a local NBC affiliate station).

11.8

LETTER

"Write a letter to the manager of a post office to explain your problem. Ask for something. Ask for help."

OR: Write to a TV station an d suggest a TV program

OR: write a letter to the editor of a newspaper

Do you know how to make a web page? There is a free program that our students at TALK use-it's called www.geocities.com. You can get a one-page list of instructions at www.geocities.com/countries2001/instruction.html

11.9

LISTENING

On the CD-1, available from www.teacherstoteachers.com, you can listen to the conversation. With your partner, listen to ten sentences, write down the entire sentences and then show the sentences to your teacher.

You can listen to some sentences by students on a videotape that is available with this book. These students are talking about their lives. Listen until you find a conversation that is interesting for you.

11.10

GRAMMAR

Write three sentences using these words:

They're, Their, There

Fill in the blank:

Where is my book?

It is _____

My two brothers are looking for _____ books.

My brothers are late. _____ sick.

11.11

READING

Subscribe to an internet e-letter and receive a new vocabulary lesson each week.

To sign up for newsletters about English Language, go here: home.about.com/newsletters1.htm

If you have any questions or comments please don't hesitate to write to the guy who directs the English.about.com web site. He can't guarantee that he'll have an answer, but chances are he'll be able to point you in the right direction.

esl.guide@about.com

For past issues of the newsletter visit The Newsletter Archive at About, 1440 Broadway 19th Floor NY, NY 10018.

11.12

JOKE

"DE" WAY TO BE (Underline the words that you don't understand)

If lawyers are disbarred and clergymen defrocked, doesn't it follow that electricians can be delighted, musicians denoted, cowboys deranged, models deposed and dry cleaners depressed?

Laundry workers could decrease, eventually becoming depressed and depleted!

Bed-makers will be debunked, baseball players will be debased, landscapers will be deflowered, bulldozer operators will be degraded, organ donors will be delivered, software engineers will be detested, the BVD company will be debriefed, and even musical composers will eventually decompose.

On a more positive note though, perhaps we can hope politicians will be devoted.

11.13
WRITE A DIALOG
Part A: Choose one of these situations and imagine the words that are said. Work with your partner.
Part B: Create another situation. Describe the situation and (if you want to) send it by e-mail to englishlesson@mail.com.

Communication
a. Fred Jones wants to buy a cell phone. Tell him that you need to ask some friends for additional information and you'll return to him with more information. (Option: do this for homework and bring literature from some local cell phone stores.)
b. Mrs. Martinez wants to send a package to her sister who lives in Peru. Can you help her? What are the options (FedEx, DHL, post office, ups??) the package weighs 20 pounds and it is 2 feet by 1 foot by 18 inches.
c. Jorge's baseball hit the satellite dish on another neighbor's roof. Mrs. Martinez called you to ask you to translate for her. The other neighbor was born in Houston, Texas.
d. Ralph hit your mail box with his car and continued to drive. He picked up the mail box and tried to make it stand straight, but it is dented and the post is broken (so it does not stand properly). You need to talk with his father.

Situation # 11. (Communication)

Celina wants to subscribe to an Internet plan, but she doesn't know which companies provide service. Which ones are the best? How much is a good price to pay per month? Is it common to use the same phone line? She asked her neighbor (who is an electronic engineer), and he told her…write an interesting conversation…if you don't know about this topic, you can interview somebody who knows.

Corrections
Nowadays, the first mass media in the whole world is, without doubt, the Internet. This is the most important technological advance that the human being has done. And it's really amazing how it has developed in a very short time.

This is something that almost nobody would have imagined 20 or 10 years ago….all the world is connected by internet, you can communicate with any person anywhere by a local call, you can buy whatever you want in the virtual stores, you can advertise your product or enterprise thru a web page, and everybody in the world can have access to it. You can obtain software, you can see and talk with people everywhere, you can take a tour and look at beautiful landscapes with animation and movement of amazing places, you can find all the information that you want about almost any topic, you can find photos, etc.

The advantages of internet are infinite and I think they are going to increase with the passing of time.

Internet is, practically, a new thing, and it allows us many things, as I mentioned before. One of the things is the free trade of everything; you can buy, sell, advertise, download music for free, etc. And all those transactions need to be legalized, so in the future it will have "internet lawyers" and a "internet constitution".

Every day it's more important the communication and the things that we do by Internet, and I think it's going to provide jobs for millions of people of any profession…more than what it's providing now.

ANSWER: Uniform Resource Locator
KSC Kennedy Space Center
NASA National Aeronautics and Space Administration
DOD Department of Defense
EVA Extra Vehicular Activity
GMT Greenwich Mean Time
JPL Jet Propulsion Laboratory
RAM Random Access Memory (the part of the computer's brain that you need for working on problems)
ROM Read-Only Memory
G gigabyte, one billion 1,000,000,000
M megabyte, one million 1,000,000
K kilobyte, one thousand 1,000

12. Teaching Techniques

12.1
PAIR WORK (CONVERSATION)
Here are some words that you need to know. Work with your partner and write a sentence with each word or phrase:
Composition
Paragraph
Essay
TTT (teacher talking time)

12.2
PAIR WORK
Work with your partner and answer these questions.
Why does the Group work together? Why doesn't the teacher talk more than 25% of the time?
Who is the most important person in the classroom?

12.3
PAIR WORK
These are suggestions for reducing the time that the teacher spends talking. Read them and decide with your partner how you can use these techniques in the next class (work with your teachers). Show these ideas to your teacher.
1. Ask the students to read the instructions for the exercises.
2. Let students explain vocabulary and grammar.

3. Let students correct other students first.

4. Let students give you examples before you give an example.

5. Ask one student to be the teacher for the class.

6. Ask the students to create their own questions and tests.

7. Ask the students to check their neighbor's written work. Then the teacher can double-check the work.

8. Don't interrupt the students when they are talking (just make notes and put the corrections on the board)

9. The teacher should pretend to have a sore throat (so students need to lead the class).

10. Ask the students to make presentations

11. Let students decide on their own discussion topics.

These ideas come from Tony Lloyd, TALK International School of Languages.

Go to this web site and see some more ideas for improving methods of teaching: www.geocities.com/stevemccrea/

For some interesting techniques for turning a boring teacher into an interesting teacher, go to www.usu.edu and click on "substitute teacher institute" and www.teacherstoteachers.com and click on "Show this to a boring teacher."

13. Stress

13.1
READING
During the holidays, there is a lot of stress.
Please visit www.geocities.com/talkinternational/dec31.html
You can read about the tradition of "holding hands with your arms crossed" that comes from England. It will be a big circle. If you are in Fort Lauderdale on Dec 31 at 11:55 pm (23.55), we hope to hold hands with you!!

Here is a student's reply
From: "Daniela Patruno" <danibabe81@hotmail.com
To: englishlesson@mail.com
Subject: Venezuelan customs on New Year's eve
The dec31 page is very good. What an interesting English tradition!! I haven´t heard it before. Here is a short composition about the Venezuelan customs on New Year's eve. Happy New Year! Please say hello to everybody at Talk, and to JK.
Daniela.

Venezuelan customs on New Year's Eve
On December 31st, we use to have a dinner, similar to the 24th one…..with pork, "hallacas", ham bread, dry figs,…etc.

At midnight, we hug each other and give them the "Happy New Year". After that, we drink a toast with champagne, and we eat 12 grapes…….you have to ask for one wish per each grape that you eat......so you have 12 wishes. Then, we go out of the house with an empty suitcase and money in the hands. You walk in the street near to your house with the suitcase, and you'll find your neighbors doing the same! The suitcase symbolize that you'll have luck to travel during the year, and the money symbolize that you'll always have money in the year. It's very funny, almost all the Venezuelan families do it.

Another custom is to use yellow underwear on that day......people say that it's for to have good luck during the next year.
Danibabe81@hotmail.com

13.2
PAIRWORK
Write to Daniela and to englishlesson@mail.com about your traditions...we'll put them on the web site for the ESL book.

13.3
PAIR WORK (CONVERSATION)
Here are some words that you need to know. Work with your partner and write a sentence with each word or phrase:
nervous
anxious
calm
uncertain
stressful

Now change these adjectives (above) and make them nouns (things).
He is worried.—> He is full of worry.

Nervous—>

Anxious—>

Calm—>

Uncertain—>

13.4
PAIRWORK
Work with your partner and answer these questions.
What do you do to reduce stress? (Breathe, exercise…?)
Is it better to "pop" a pimple or to put medication on the pimple?

13.5
ADVICE: Hre is an exercise. Put the words in the sentences below.
"It's a good idea to…"
walk deeply smile
_____ and think about a positive place.
Breathe _____.
Go for a _____.

It's a good idea to look for the caveman or the cavewoman inside you.
A guy named Rob Becker created a funny one-man show. You can see
some   of   his   comments   at   www.caveman.com   and   at
www.angelfire.com/fl4/cavemanwoman—The cavewoman looks for
protection and she chooses the man in her life to protect her future
children. The caveman wants to protect his group from danger and he
knows how to hunt (so he can don one thing at a time). A caveman
who does two things at once is under stress. A cavewoman who is
asked to ignore her desire to create harmony is under stress. By watching the caveman or cavewoman inside you, you can understand why
you feel stress.

After you read the web site, ask your partner to decide "True" or "False" (below):

A caveman likes to clean and organize his cave because then he can find the rabbits that are hiding in the cave. TRUE or FALSE

A cavewoman can look at another cave without thinking about moving to the new cave. TRUE or FALSE

A caveman enjoyed looking around him when he was hunting, looking for other animals to chase. TRUE or FALSE

A caveman likes to do one thing at a time. TRUE or FALSE

A cavewoman can cook, listen to her baby and watch what is happening outside the cave. TRUE or FALSE

In Chapter 5 of this book, there is similar information about men and women and a website (www.geocities.com/talkinternational/menand-women.html).

13.6
LAUGH
One of the most stressful relationships in life is between men and women. A good way to deal with stress is to laugh!

Knowing women's minds
The Men's Guide to what a woman really means when she says…

What she says = what she is thinking
"I need" = "I want"
"It's your decision" = "The correct decision should be obvious by now"

"Do what you want" = "You'll pay for this later"

"Fine" = "You'll pay for this later."

"We need to talk" = "I need to complain."

"I'm not upset" = "Of course I'm upset, you moron!"

"You're so manly" = "You need a shave and you sweat a lot."

"Be romantic, turn out the lights" = "I have flabby things."

"This kitchen is so inconvenient" = "I want a new house."

"I need wedding shoes" = "The other 40 pairs are the wrong shade of white."

"Hang the picture there" = "NO, I mean hang it there!"

"I heard a noise" = "I noticed you were almost asleep."

"Do you love me?" = "I'm going to ask for something expensive."

"How much do you love me?" = "I did something today you're really not going to like."

"I'll be ready in a minute" = "Kick off your shoes and find a good game on TV."

"Is my butt fat?" = "Tell me I'm beautiful."

"You have to learn to communicate" = "Just agree with me."

"Are you listening to me!?" = "Too late, you're dead."

"Do you like this recipe?" = "It's easy to fix, so you'd better get used to it."

"I'm not yelling!" = "Yes, I am yelling because I think this is important."

WITH YOUR PARTNER

Do you agree with these jokes? Here's an exercise: with your partner, write similar jokes for "How to understand the man's mind." Send your ideas to *englishlesson@mail.com.*

13.7

INTERNET: Here are some internet sites for you to visit to find more information. (If you know about other web sites, please send a message to englishlesson@mail.com and we will consider adding your suggestion to our web site.) Go to www.realage.com then type "stress reduction" in the SEARCH box.

13.8

READING: Subscribe to an internet e-letter and receive a new vocabulary lesson each week. Here's a suggestion: Go to *www.nytimes.com/subscribe* and enter your e-mail address. You will receive this message:

This is a special offer from The New York Times Circulation. ABOUT THIS E-MAIL: Your registration to NYTimes.com included permission to send you occasional e-mail with special offers from our advertisers. As a member of the BBBOnline Privacy Program and the TRUSTe privacy program, we are committed to protecting your privacy; to unsubscribe from future mailings, visit *www.nytimes.com/unsubscribe*. Suggestions and feedback are welcome at comments@nytimes.com

13.9

JOKE

Work with your partner to find problems of grammar. Also underline the words that are difficult for you and ask your teacher to explain the new words.

The White House didn't just get a new team, but a whole new language. George W. Bush has brought with him many friends from Texas, and for anyone not born in the Lone Star State, the Texas accent and the

cowboy colloquialisms can seem a bit strange. Here is a guide to a few of the more colorful expressions they will encounter:

1. The engine's runnin' but ain't nobody driving
The person is not overly intelligent.

2. As welcome as a skunk at a lawn party

(self-explanatory).

3. Tighter than bark on a tree
Not very generous.

4. Big hat, no cattle
All talk and no action.

5. It's so dry the trees are bribin' the dogs
We really could use a little rain around here.

6. Just because a chicken's got wings don't mean it can fly
Appearances can be deceptive.

7. You can put your boots in the oven, but that don't make them bis-
cuits
You can say whatever you want about something, but that doesn't
change the facts.

Resources

Evaluation Sheet for a Speaking Test (a focus on Pronunciation and Grammar)

Suggestion Sheet (to tell the students about their progress and to give the students a list of things to work on and practice)

Evaluation Sheet for a Speaking Test

This worksheet is a focus on Pronunciation and Grammar.

Name of the Speaker: _____

Did the speaker miss the ends of words? (give an example)

Was the speaker clear? Did the speaker speak clearly?

Circle the vowel sounds that the speaker missed (and give an example)
EXAMPLE SUN the speaker said "coot" like "moon" (cut)

Day	See	Write	Go	Moon
Cat	Pen	Fish	Shop	Sun

_____

Dog

House

Foot

Grammar Errors (example)
Error: He have a son (correct: he has a son)

Error: He did not found his keys (correct: he did not find his keys)

Did the speaker appear confident? Did the speaker pause or speak too slowly?

Can you suggest something to the speaker?

Do you have other comments?

Suggestion Sheet

This sheet asks, "What do you need to work on?" After you complete this sheet, you will know!

Student: _____ Date: _____

Advisor _____

Pronunciation

Late Said Sit bit site right fight bite straight grow now know show snow allow

Two through thought through rough bed head bread Yesterday I read a book.

Think thing thin that this these those thin thick bath breath bread breathe

Talk all cat cloud jaw smile jump pause fight straight eight neighbor receive

Writing

Speaking

Listening

Here's what I want you to do to improve:

Bring a video to class.

Listen to a cassette and repeat the words.

Teach a page from a picture dictionary to the class.

Write a composition.

Comments:

More Letters

WORK WITH YOUR PARTNER: What are the reasons for writing letters?

1.
_____

2.
_____

3.
_____

4.
_____

(Some answers are on the next page)

The basic structure of a letter

1. start with a nice opening. Get the person's attention
2. Introduce yourself quickly.
3. give the background information
4. quickly get to the purpose of the letter

5. say something nice about the person. (optional)

Samples:
"I know that you must be busy at this time of year. I hope you can help me."
(You can write this sentence to almost any government agency.... Those workers are usually overworked.)

Answers
There are many reasons for writing letters.

1. To complain. 2. To give comfort. 3. To request information. 4. To ask for help. Can you think of other reasons? Congratulate, praise, make a suggestion...

Holidays

The Exercise: With your partner write a few sentences to describe each of these holidays. If you don't know when it happens or why it is observed, you can skip it (jump over it) and you can ask the teacher or other groups to explain the holiday. Decide with your partner if the banks are closed on these holidays.

New Year's Day
Martin Luther King, Jr. Day
President's Day
St. Patrick's Day
Memorial Day
Flag Day
The Fourth of July
Bastille Day
Labor Day
Rosh Hashanah
Columbus Day
Veterans' Day
Thanksgiving
Christmas

ANSWERS
A * in front of the day indicates that banks and government offices are closed on this holiday.

*New Year's Day (January 1) ++ is a holiday.

*Martin Luther King, Jr. Day is usually on the Monday that is close to January 16, the birthday of the civil rights leader. It is usually the third Monday in January.

*President's Day (February) is usually held around February 22, near the birthdays of Lincoln and George Washington.

St. Patrick's Day (March 17) is not an observed holiday in most parts of the USA, but a lot of pubs celebrate, usually the weekend before March 17. There is a famous parade on the 17th and New York City usually "shuts down."

*Memorial Day (the fourth weekend in May) helps us remember the men who died in wars.

Flag Day (June 14) is not an official holiday but it's a good reason to put a flag outside your house.

*The Fourth of July ++ is the day of U.S. independence (although the actual document was signed over three or four days, according to historians).

Bastille Day (July 14) is the independence day of France. (It is not an official U.S. holiday but many people like to remember Lafayette, the general who helped in the fight against the King of England.)

*Labor Day (The Monday after the first Saturday in September) lets us remember the labor unions that worked to protect workers. In 1870, the typical person worked 12 hours 6 days a week. Now we work 8 hours 5 days a week.

Rosh Hashanah is observed by Jews. Nova University is usually closed.

*Columbus Day (October 12) ++ is a bank holiday but is considered by some people to be a date that remembers the voyager but not the suffering of the natives who later died from diseases brought by Columbus' men.

Veterans' Day occurs in early November (usually around Nov. 11, which as the day when World War 1 ended in 1918). We remember veterans of wars who suffered and who are still with us.

*Thanksgiving (the fourth Thursday in November) reminds us of the time when some immigrants from England moved to Plymouth, Massachusetts and they received help from the local people.

*Christmas ++ is on December 25.

++Note: if the date falls on a Saturday, there is sometimes a holiday on Friday. If the date falls on a Sunday, then the holiday is observed on Monday.

Words to Songs (Lyrics) for Christmas and Songs for Irish and English Pubs
There are numerous web sites where you can find the words to songs. A list of them appears on www.geocities.com/talkinternational/holidays.html.

PART B "Interesting Little Topics" from A to Z

TO THE READER
In this section you will find small pieces of advice, little suggestions, bits of cultural information. Do not try to memorize these items. They are for your enjoyment. The words are not in alphabetical order within each category of letter.

If you learn about something and you want to tell other students about it (or if you have a question about a little topic), please send your advice or suggestion to: englishlesson@mail.com and make the SUBJECT of your e-mail like this: "For the A to Z section of the ESL book." (This will tell me to put your comments in the A-Z website). There is space at the end of each section of this Alphabet to give you some room to write your special vocabulary words. Many of them are suggested by Roxana Larrazabal.

Look for your suggestion in our website at www.geocities.com/countries/esl.html.

Visit this web site for more information that was submitted by students: www.geocities.com/talkinternational/atoz.html

For a special web site, created with advice from Roxana, please see www.geocities.com/talkinternational/roxana.html (We put in a few mistakes to confuse you. Look carefully! Answers are on the web site)

-A-
ADD-Attention Deficit Disorder (where the child has a difficult time focusing.
ASAP-As soon as possible.
ALBERTSONS-A big supermarket.
AOL-America Online. It's an internet supplier.
AVENTURA MALL-A big mall in Miami Beach.
ALIKE-When something is equal.
A LOT-An informal way to say a large number or amount.
AT ODDS-When there is a conflict or disagreement, opposed.

-B-
BTW-By the way.
BELLSOUTH-A big company, phone and internet supplier.
BRB-Be right back.
BEST BUY-The lowest prices for all types of electronics.
BE MY GUEST-Feel free to use it.
BACK OUT-When you brake a promise or an agree.
BAD PAPER-When you give a check, and it doesn't have any found.
BED OF ROSES-When you have an easy life…your job is pleasant.
BREAK WITH-When you separate oneself from / end member ship.
BRING OFF-To do something difficult / to perform successfully.

-C-

CAR MAX-It's the biggest car dealership in South Florida.

CASINOS-There are casinos on Indian reservations and on cruise ships. The ships "go nowhere" (about 12 miles away from land) and the gambling machines are turned on.

CATS-www.browardhumane.com/cats.html Go to the website and learn about keeping pets. You can see lots of cat photos at www.allthe-cats.com.

COSTCO-It's a big store where you can buy food wholesale, and you can also buy clothes, to develop photos, etc. But you need a card that you can obtain there.

CO-PAYMENT-A minimum payment that you do when you belong to a medical program.

CATEGORY-A group of things that are alike.

CALL NAMES-When you use an ugly word to speak with or about someone.

CANOT AND STICK-You use this when your son brought bad grades. It's the promise of reward and threat of punishment.

-D-

DAVE AND BUSTER'S-A place in Hollywood, with interactive games, billiards and food….it's very fun.

DEATH-How much does it cost to bury a body? (About $3,000). How much for cremation? (About $800).

DENNYS-A restaurant with American food, opened 24 hours.

DENTIST-Do you need a dentist? Visit Nova University's center and get a recommendation.

DISNEY-Here's a suggestion: go to Disney Quest and avoid the crowds in the parks.

DOGS-You can find lots of photos about dogs at www.dogomania.com.

DRIVER LICENSE-You can practice at www.quia.com/ and you can find information about the driver license requirements by going to www.yahoo.com then type "Driver License Florida" and click on SEARCH. One of the links will be the state of Florida's site: www.hsmv.state.fl.us/html/dlnew.html Click on the "ONLINE TRAFFIC TEST" in the lower left corner of the web page.

DRAFT-First copy.

DETAILS-They are important when you write riddles.

DIG UP-To find or get something with some effort.

DO AWAY WITH-To put and end something / to stop.

DASH OFF-To make, do or finish quickly, specially when you draw, paint or write hurriedly.

DOPE OUT-When you are thinking of something to explain.

-E-

ECKERD-A store where you can buy drugs, cosmetics and other things.

ENVIRONMENTAL GROUPS-There are many organizations that are not-for-profit and that protect the environment. It is a tradition in the USA for individuals to support organizations that support nature. One of the most influential organizations is the Sierra Club. www.sierra-club.org. Others include the Manatee clubs (see M for manatees).

EVERGLADES-A touristic place where you can see alligators, you have airboats tours, fishing, boat rentals, campground, etc.

ETA-A terrorist group who want to separate Spain of France.

EASY DOES IT-Let's do it carefully, without sudden movements and without forcing it too hard or fast.

EYES POP OUT-When you have a big surprise.

-F-

FIRST UNION-A popular bank.

FIU-Florida International University.

FAU-Florida Atlantic University.

FASHION MALL-A big mall in University Dr, in Plantation. 321 N.

FOOD-www.everythingaboutfood.com (it's a great web site)

FPL-Florida Power Light, the company that supplies electricity for the Florida State.

FALL BACK-To move back, go back.

FALL BEHIND-To go slower than others and be far behind them.

FAT CHANCE-When you have a little possibility, almost no chance.

-G-

GAS STATIONS-You have to put gas by yourself, because there is not any petrol-pump.

GRAND PRIX RACE-O-RAMA-An amusement park, located on I-95 E.

GRAPEFRUIT-Eat the white part, it is good for you and has fiber.

GROCERIES-Another name for "food". A grocery store = a small supermarket.

GAIN GROUND-To go forward, more ahead.

GET AHEAD-To become successful.

GET AT-To reach an understanding. (When some book is very hard to understand).

GET BACK AT-When you do something bad to hurt in return.

GET SET-To get ready to start.
GET WITH IT-To pay attention, be alive or alert, get busy.

-H-
HOME DEPOT-A big store where you will find everything for your house, from a spoon to wood pieces to build houses.
HIGH STYLE-A beautiful furniture store in North Miami Beach, with many modern furniture.
HUDDLE-Crowd together. Number of people or things close together.
HUNCH-Idea based on a feeling. When you feel that something is happening or something is going to happen.
HURRICANE-Storm with very string winds.
HANG IT-An exclamation used to express disappointment.
HAVE AN EDGE ON-To have an advantage.
HIT IT OFF-To enjoy with another's company, to be happy and comfortable in each other's presence.

-I-
I.O.U.-I owe you. It's something that you sign when you owe money to someone.
INDIANS-They are called Native Americans. There are Seminoles and Miccosukee in South Florida. They operate casinos.
ILL AT EASE-Not feeling at ease or comfortable when you are worried, unhappy.
IN A CIRCLE, OR IN CIRCLES-When there is not any progress.
IN THE CLOUDS-When you are far from real life.

-J-

JAI-ALAI-A game played with a basket and a ball that is bounced off a wall. There's a good Jai-Alai game arena in Dania Beach.

JUICE-The best oranges for juice are available between January 15 and February 28, usually. These oranges come from Indian River, north of West Palm Beach.

JUMP DOWN ONE'S THOUGHT-When you suddenly become very angry with someone.

JUMP TO A CONCLUSION-When you decide something to quickly or without thinking or binding the facts.

JUST SO-When you must have great care, very careful.

-K-

KEYWEST-You can visit Key West any time of the year, but the least crowded time is in the Summer. You can go on line and see photos made by students at www.virtourist.com and click on AMERICAS and then KEY WEST-There is a virtual tour at www.virtualkeywest.com

KOSHER-Food that is approved for Jewish religious use.

KEEP AFTER-When you speak with someone about something several times, again, again, and again (repeat).

KEEP ON-To go ahead, not to stop, continue.

KEEP AT-To continue doing….

-L-

LAWN-The green grass around your home.

LEASE-A way for renting a car for two or three years.

LOTTO-The name of the Lottery in Florida.

LABOR OF LOVE-When you do something for personal pleasant, without payment or profit.

LEAD OFF-To begin, to start, open.

LACK-When you don't have enough. When you need courage.

-M-

MANATEES-Visit some of the web sites that are associated with manatees. www.miamiseaquarium.com Miami Seaquarium works to rescue injured manatees. Homosassa Springs State Park is a wonderful place to see manatees. (352) 628-5343. Save the Manatee Club, 1-800-432-JOIN. Manatee Survival Foundation, 954-943-4391.

MEATBALL-Small round ball made with meat.

MEASURE-System for calculating amounts, size, weight, etc.

MIX UP-When you are confused, make a mistake about something.

MONEY TO BURN-When you have a lot of money, it's more than you need, so you have money to burn.

-N-
NATURAL FOODS-There are stores that sell food without preservatives and pesticides. Two of the stores are called Wild Oats and Bread of Life.
NOBODY'S FOOL-Person who knows what is he/she doing. He/she can take care of themselves.
NEVER MIND-Don't worry about it, forget it.
NERVOUS NELLIE-It means a timid person who leaches determination and courage.

-O-
ORLANDO-If you are looking for a list of recommendations, www.orlando.com.
OFF GUARD-Not alert to the unexpected.
ONCE OVER-When you look quickly on examination of someone or something.

-P-
PARKING-If you are willing to walk, you can often find low-cost parking. If you go to www.geocities.com/talkinternatinal/parking.html, you can see a list of Steve's favorite parking spots in Miami, Fort Lauderdale and West Palm Beach.
PETS-Visit this web site and learn about what you should do to keep your pets happy. Click on DOGS or CATS-www.browardhumane.com/ouranfrien.html

PIER-The places where you can walk over the water and fish. Broward has four piers: Dania, Lauderdale By the Sea (Commercial Blvd.), Pompano (north of Atlantic) and Deerfield Beach.

POLITICAL LEADERS-RFK, JFK, LBJ, FDR, TR, RR

PARAGRAPH-Group of details sentences that tell you about on main idea.

PULL OVER-When you drive to the side on the road and stop.

PULL THE PLUG ON-When you expos secret activities.

-Q-

QUOTES-What is your favorite quotation? "Fake it until you make it." Or "If you can see it, you can be it."

QUARREL-Fight, argument, cause for a disagreement.

QUIZ-Game, competition where the questions are put. To ask questions of someone.

-R-

RANDOM ACTS OF KINDNESS-There is an expression that started in California. Some "random acts of violence" were made by some bad people, so some good people started to help strangers. When they went through a toll, they paid for the car behind them. They put money in a parking meter that was about to expire. They called the acts "random acts of kindness."

RULES for late students-Do not knock on the classroom door. Do not smile and say "Hi!" or "Sorry I'm late" because your voice will interrupt the class.

RING A BELL-To make one remember.

RING DOWN-When you have poor health or condition. Weak on needing much work.

.

-S-

SHOWER HEAD-Someone once told me that germs grow in the shower head. It's a good idea to remove the head and soak it in chlorine at least once a year to kill bacteria that sit in it.

SUNPASS-There are special lanes in the toll system that give you a fast way to pay the toll on the turnpike. You can learn more by calling 1-888-TOLL-FLA or 1-888-_ _ _-_ _ _ _. What are the numbers that go with these letters? The answer is at the end of this chapter.

SUNSET-the best views of the sunsets in South Florida are in Naples (2 hours from Fort Lauderdale) and Key West.

SAM'S-Big store where you can find groceries, appliances for your house, your car, clothes, etc.

SEQUENCE-Tells what comes first, next, and last.

SLOPPY-When something looks informal, careless or dirty.

SLOB-Means rude, lazy or carelessly.

SUDDENLY-When something happens quickly and unexpectedly.

-T-

TELEPHONE ALPHABET-When you speak on the telephone and you spell a street name or your last name, use the names of children or cities: "DESOTA, D David, E Elephant, S Sam, O Orlando, T Thomas and A apple"

TEST-You can test yourself online at www.quia.com/ and you can select ENGLISH or CHEMISTRY or any subject…even driver's education.

THREAT-You promise to do something. "If you don't do it, you will have a punishment".

TAKE OVER-When you take control or possession of….

THINK OVER-When you think carefully about something, to consider, to study.

-U-

UMBRELLA-You need to carry one in your car…you never know when it will storm in South Florida.

UPHOLSTERY-If you have a rip in your chair, you need to look up this word to find a company to repair the cushion.

UNEXPECTEDLY-When something that is not supposed to happen, occur.

-V-

VINEGAR-www.everythingaboutfood.com/ph_acid_food_0906.htm You can go here and learn about acid and alkaline in your foods. Vinegar is an acid.

VARIETY SHOW-Program that includes several different kind of entertainment.

VERY WELL-Used to show agreement or approval.

VOTE DOWN-When someone defeat in a vote.

-W-

WATER-The water in South Florida is not very good! The water has a bad taste and many residents use filters to reduce the taste of chlorine. The water in 8000 municipalities in the USA violated safe drinking water laws at some point in 1998, according to a study. Check your yellow pages for a good system. In Dade County, the local government sells a $200 filter that works well: Carbostar, distributed by South Dade Soil and Water Conservation District, 305.242.1288, 305.242.1292 fax, sodadeswcd@aol.com.

WATER TAXI-A fun way to get around Miami and Fort Lauderdale. www.watertaxi.com.

WITNESS-A person who is present when something happens.

WHAT WITH-Means because, as a result of.

WHIP UP-When you do something quickly or easily.

-X-

X-RAY-It's the best way to say "X like X-ray" (the telephone alphabet).

XEROX-A form of photocopying.

XERISCAPE-You use plants that don't need a lot of water. Usually these are plants that are native to the region. "xeri" = dry.

-Y-

YACHT-Large sailboats and motorboats.

YELLOW BELLIED-Slang for say somebody extremely timid cow-ardly.

YES MAN-Person who tries to be liked, always trying to agree with everybody, especially a boss.

-Z-

ZOO-Where is a good zoo in South Florida? (Give your opinion if you have one.) Metro Zoo in Miami, Butterfly World in Broward and Lion Country Safari and Dreher Park Zoo in West Palm Beach.

1-888-TOLL-FLA or 1-888-_ _ _-_ _ _ _. Look at a telephone. What are the letters under the numbers? 2 = ABC, 3 = DEF, 4 = GHI, 5 = JKL, 6 = MNO, 7 = PQRS, 8 = TUV, 9 = WXYZ. So the TOLL-FLA number is 1-888-8655-352.

Remember, for more items (and to get updated advice), visit this web site for more information that was submitted by students: www.geoci-ties.com/talkinternational/atoz.html.

CD-roms are available from
www.teacherstoteachers.com

NOTE TO TEACHERS: You can use these videos in the CD to extend the lessons in this book. In each chapter, one of the videos below can be duplicated and distributed to the class. On one CD you have enough video material for plenty of classroom discussion.

Please look for the name of the video that you want to watch.

Each video has numbers showing the time of the video. If you click on the right number, such as 1:31, or one minute and 31 seconds, you will see a part of the video that talks about a special subject. I put a summary of each part of each video in the area below here. (I want to thank Kumi and Sharon Pi-Ying for these suggestions. It is a good idea to give the students a summary of the conversation and a summary of the parts of each conversation.)

I suggest that you will find it interesting to write the transcript WORD FOR WORD and send it to me. Please visit www.teacherstoteachers.com to see if there is a transcript already in place on the web site (for you to check your writing).

Please remember that the purpose of these videos is to encourage you to listen closely and practice spelling. You should LISTEN to one sentence, STOP the video, WRITE the sentence, GO BACK and check the pronunciation, then CONTINUE. It will be slow but you will discover that you have many words that you don't know. You can go to the transcripts section of www.teacherstoteachers.com to find the exact words (after students submit their transcripts). I will do the first one and I hope my students will do the rest (and I will check their spelling).

Good luck! Please send comments to *englishlesson@mail.com*.

Rules in the Classroom

1. Class starts at 9 a.m.

2. Good students arrive at class before 9 a.m. so that they are ready to learn. Good students are in their seats at 8:59 a.m.

3. If you are late, go to the administration office and explain why you are late. If it is a good excuse, she will give you a piece of paper to confirm that you have a good excuse. Give the piece of paper to your teacher. The teacher will mark you as E, excused.

4. If you are late by more than 15 minutes (past 9:15 a.m.), do not go to class. Study in another room until the next class starts at 11 a.m. If you are late two times in the same week by more than 15 minutes, you will have one A absent on your attendance list.

5. Students on a student visa (I-20) must attend at least 80% of the classes. Please see Mari for all of the rules related to attendance.

6. If you miss the class, call the teacher to get the homework.

7. The Rule of 34: Several studies measured how fast a group of students learned 100 words. The first group spoke ONLY ENGLISH in the classroom. All explanations were in English. The second group sometimes allowed students to talk in another language in the class. The first group took 10 weeks to learn the 100 words. The second group took 13.4 weeks to learn the same 100 words. Conclusion: it will take you 34% longer if you don't speak English in the classroom.

Steve's additional rules:
If you are late, walk quietly into the room.
Do not say, "I'm sorry."
Do not explain why you are late.

Do not disturb the class.
Do not knock on the door.
Open the door quietly and slip into the room like a thief. You are invisible to me if you are late. Students who are on time get special prizes.

If Steve is late, please work together to agree on the next thing to do. Check your homework. Look in the FIVE-MINUTE ACTVITIES BOOK

If you need to make a telephone call or go outside the classroom, do not ask the teacher if it is OK to leave the room. Just go and be quiet.

If your cell phone rings, leave the room and answer it. Do not speak on the mobile telephone in the classroom.

Epilogue

Thank you for reading this book.

Now it is time for you to write a letter to someone and practice asking questions. Make a suggestion. Send more materials for the web site at *www.teacherstoteachers.com.*

Please register for updates to this book. We will send you the updates automatically to alert you that there is new material on the ESL web sites. Please send your e-mail address to englishlesson@mail.com.

You can start with the students who wrote this book. Write to them and tell them something positive about the book and make a suggestion to improve the book.

For example, write to danibabe81@hotmail.com and thank her for typing the majority of the compositions that appeared in this book.

Bye! We wish you success in the USA!

About the Author

Steve McCrea is a teacher at TALK International School of Languages in Fort Lauderdale. Please visit the web site at *www.talkinusa.com* for more information.

For a list of other teaching and learning tools, visit these web sites:

www.whatdoyaknow.com

www.teacherstoteachers.com

Printed in the United States
26747LVS00002B/331